The Presenter's Handbook

How to give a captivating performance – **Every time!**

© Phillip Adcock & Ian Callow

February 2012

The Presenter's Handbook

How to Give a Captivating Performance –

Every Time!

by

Phillip Adcock and Ian Callow

ISBN: 978-0-9571909-0-0

Published by The Presenter's Handbook Press in conjunction with Writersworld. This book is produced entirely in the UK, is available to order from most bookshops in the United Kingdom, and is globally available via UK-based Internet book retailers.

Copy edited by Ian Large

Cover design Jag Lall

WRITERSWORLD
2 Bear Close Flats
Bear Close
Woodstock
Oxfordshire
OX20 1JX
England

www.writersworld.co.uk

The text pages of this book are produced via an independent certification process that ensures the trees from which the paper is produced come from well-managed sources that exclude the risk of using illegally logged timber while leaving options to use post-consumer recycled paper as well.

Also by Phillip Adcock: **Supermarket Shoppology** – *The science of supermarket shopping… …and a strategy to spend less and get more.*

Hardback: ISBN 978-0-9569564-2-2

Paperback: ISBN 978-0-9569564-0-8

Also available as an e-book

The Presenter's Handbook

How to give a captivating performance – **Every time!**

Contents

Section 3 Your performance 153

Section 4 Final thoughts 237

Acknowledgements

As we began to think about all the people whom we should thank for their input and support to make this book possible, the list just grew and grew. So, Phillip and Ian have decided to each acknowledge different people.

Phillip would like to thank his wife, Kay, and daughter, Amy, for continuing to inspire him to work on this project day and night, month after month.

Next, he would like to thank his auntie Sylvia Jones, who many years ago gave him one of those 'get anything you want' self-help books. This book introduced him to the subject of the human brain, for which he will always remain deeply indebted.

He would also like to thank the great and the good in academia for their continual advancements in the understanding of how human beings operate, in particular, Robert Plutchik, Steven Pinker and Antonio Damasio. He is also grateful that their work is so accessible.

Special thanks must go to the team at Shopping Behaviour Xplained Ltd who continually push the boundaries of human understanding by converting shopper research insights into communication tactics and strategies that drive sales and increase customer satisfaction.

Finally, to all those science teachers who make this fascinating subject of human psychology so boring and irrelevant to teenagers: Change. Change the way you teach, spice it up. There is nothing more exciting and inspiring than understanding how we as a species operate, how we communicate with each other and why we are what we are.

Ian (@idcallow) would like to thank his supportive family of his wife, Dawn, and his children, Shona and Cameron. They have all offered support and understanding during his time writing chapters of this book and supporting training materials.

He also offers a big thank you to those companies who have supported him during his training and presenting career, especially Mitt Nathwani and Frances Williams from TurningTechnologiesUK (@turningtechuk); Marika Bojmalieva, Kerri Staff and Michelle Evans from Steljes Limited (@SteljesGroup) in conjunction with @SMART_tech; and everyone connected to iconnect2learn. All of these companies continue to provide inspirational products for management productivity and professional development.

Ian works with all of those companies to perform training and presentations. Providing professional development to clients and receiving quality feedback provides a source of continued inspiration for him.

A joint thank you goes to the game of golf for introducing Phillip and Ian, without which this book and training modules may have remained unwritten.

Introduction

"The single biggest problem in communication is the illusion that it has taken place."
George Bernard Shaw

It is estimated that there are 30,000,000 PowerPoint presentations created every single day (Ian Parker, The New Yorker). That's a lot of slides. This Microsoft software application has become a core communication tool within so many walks of life. Whether it's the business-to-business presentation, the college lecture or even the Sunday sermon at church, PowerPoint is in there, visualising what speakers are talking about. The program is supposed to help both the speaker with easier access to his subject matter and the participants with visual information, which complements what is being said by the speaker.

But if so much communication relies on PowerPoint to enhance and build on the spoken message, why do so many presentations fail to engage their audiences? What is it about the sight of a presenter firing up their presentation on a computer that so effectively causes so many audiences to roll their eyes and disengage pretty much immediately?

PowerPoint is a great presentation aid and is able to transform even the most boring subject (and presenter) into an engaging and informative event, but for a large proportion of presentations, the cold hard fact is that it doesn't. But hey, don't get all antsy with the software because it isn't PowerPoint that's to blame, but the way it is used; and that is what this book is all about.

If you want your presentation to get your key message across to the audience immeasurably more effectively, then this book is designed for you. Whether you are selling, educating, informing, sharing or even preaching, the contents of the coming pages will transform your presentation skills and communication ability, starting immediately. Once you've read and digested extracts from the forthcoming pages (or better still, the whole book), you'll be able to powerfully apply the lessons not only when you present, but in many other communications-related aspects of your life; in fact pretty much any time that you communicate with other human beings face to face. I know that may sound like a bold claim to make, but trust us as it is absolutely true!

Let's begin by defining the meaning of the word communication (in relation to human-to-human communication that is). According to *Wikipedia*: *"Communication is the activity of conveying information. Communication has been derived from the Latin word* communis, *meaning 'to share'. Communication requires a sender, a message, and an intended recipient (or group of recipients)."* They also define presentation as *"the practice of showing and explaining the content of a topic to an audience or learner"*. You'll see that the two words 'communication' and 'presentation' can have very similar meanings and that is the very essence of what this book is all about. It aims to explain and educate, describe and illustrate how almost anyone can become a more effective communicator – A real Power Presenter.

Although there are many, many books on PowerPoint and even more on public speaking, our research has identified a dearth of titles that bring the two together; particularly in respect of the effectiveness of the communication being presented and received. Again, that is why this book has been written. As modern day philosopher Alain De Botton said, *"I passionately believe that it's not just what you say that counts, it's also how you say it – that the success of your argument critically depends on your manner of presenting it."*

How this book works

In the first section of the book, we're going to concentrate on you as a presenter. Forget the support you have in terms of presentation aids, technology, and even PowerPoint. This is all about you! Firstly, find out why you have less than 30 seconds interacting with others before they have formed their opinion of you (first impressions really do count). And that those 30 seconds may well be nothing to do with your time on stage. Next you'll be introduced to one of the most amazing breakthroughs in modern psychology – mirror neurons. Find out what they are and how they can be such a powerful ally to you as a presenter. The book then goes on to explore a number of other mental aspects relevant to us as presenters and presenting: These include anchoring, non-verbal communication (intended and unavoidable), human language itself and something known as 'representational systems', more about which we'll explain later.

The first section of the book is all about maximising the impact and effectiveness of you as a presenter. You are the living link between the audience and the subject matter, including those all important key messages. It is your role to manage the audience and key message relationships in order to optimise the communication from presentation to audience. This book is here to help you do this more effectively and to help your communication to have more impact.

The second section of the book moves on to the presentation's itself. We begin by looking at how you can theme and tone your presentation to better match the type of content and information you are communicating. Then we go on to explain that human brains are notoriously poor at remembering things (particularly in an educational context), and that the more you say/spray, the less the audience are likely to take on board.

We discuss some key time-related considerations that need to be considered if you want to ensure a clear and concise presentation.

How long is the presentation? How long should it be for? What if I over- or under-run?

Having covered aspects of presentational tone and style, the book goes on to explore the relationship between the presenter and the audience – How well do they know each other and what does this mean to the presentation?

Then the book takes an important step backwards; millions and millions of years to be precise and discusses our very evolution. It describes what evolution is and how it moulds and shapes much of our communication with each other. For example, did you know that visual images have been processed by human brains and their evolutionary predecessors for around 10,000 times as long as language and words have been around? So why is it that, in light of this evolutionary limitation, so much PowerPoint communication relies on words to communicate? We'll explain how and why it shouldn't; plus we'll provide some better and more effective ways to get your points across.

Then there is another deeply rooted aspect of human psychology. Emotion – without which pretty much any presentation is a failure. The book goes on to explain that it is impossible to escape the fact that as human beings, we are emotional. In fact, almost every decision that we make, we do so emotionally and not rationally. So as you sit in an audience absorbing a presentation, you are constantly filtering the contents, including how it is delivered, through your own emotions. Discover why understanding and working with the emotions of the audience are absolutely pivotal to all Power Presenters.

After explaining why the human brain is very limited in its ability to process information (including presentations), we focus on the matter of building slides; this relates to being able to build a slide to let the story unfold, as opposed to just going 'splat' – there it all is.

Next, and this may come as a shock to many, the book attempts to persuade readers just how inappropriate bullet points are in almost any presentation. We demonstrate, using evidence and expert opinion, how bad and inappropriate those apparently innocuous, but so easy and convenient to use, bullet points are.

In Section 3, the book moves on to the subject of your performance: Bringing you as a presenter and your content, the presentation, together in order to deliver a performance and really convey and communicate with the audience effectively. To start with, we explore the relevance of how your presentation fits into any bigger series of presentations. For example, you may be providing a 30-minute talk during a three-day conference. We even ask you to consider where your presentation sits within that day of the audience's lives (hmm, there's something to think about).

The next chapter goes on to investigate the influence that breaks have on delegates. Are they looking forward to the next break or have they just had one and need re-engaging? We also discuss how much you can and should move around on the stage to optimise audience engagement and offer a wealth of practical advice regarding making the most of the venue surroundings.

Then we look in detail at probably the most important aspect of the design and creation of a good presentation. If there is one single thing that will help most of us have the confidence to deliver the best presentation we can, it's having the confidence in our own ability to do so. We'll demonstrate to you how to be more confident, much more confident throughout the pages of this book.

Then we go on to explain that as a Power Presenter, you have four powerful tools at your disposal and each is discussed individually.

Finally, in Section 4, we turn our attention to various aspects related to reviewing and analysing each presentation you give as part of your development as a Power Presenter.

In the first chapter we explore simple ways that you can analyse your own presentation; from recruiting the help of colleagues to the use of electronic aids such as video cameras and electronic voting devices.

Next we move on to discuss what happens immediately after you deliver your presentation. If you are committed to being absolutely the best presenter you can, then you need to continually learn and develop. And here we offer some techniques you should consider using. We cover self-analysis, employing the services of a friend or colleague and even ways in which you can get professional presentation design and delivery analysis. We ask the question, of what feedback do you look for? Do you have any structure for receiving feedback or is it just left to chance? We summarise a number of options that again we think you ought to consider.

We can't overemphasize enough the importance of making your presentation as good as it can be, and if not this one then improve with the next one, and the next one, and so on. All too often, so much hangs on how well the presentation goes and yet presenters seem to think that a few slides loaded with bullet points are enough to do the trick. In our opinion, this should never, ever be the case! Our evidence suggests that the value of the opportunity each presentation offers is all too often severely underestimated when it comes to deciding how much time, effort and sometimes financial investment is allocated into its creation and delivery. This we fundamentally think is completely false economy and so, rightly unjustifiable.

If you ever have to present and are serious about wanting to do it well, then we implore you to read on.

Section 1

You as a presenter

Introduction

"I don't think anything is unrealistic if you believe you can do it."
Richard L. Evans

To begin with, ask yourself a question: "What is the difference between an email, a letter, a written proposal and a live presentation event?" Typically the presentation involves somebody presenting the information, whereas the others rely on the recipients reading the messages. Therefore, the presenter has a key role to play in the delivery of a presentation and, more often than not, the importance of their input is significantly underestimated.

Not here! This entire section is focussed all around how you the presenter can enhance the presentation and more effectively communicate key messages to an audience in both an engaging and memorable manner.

In this first section of the book, we're going to concentrate on you as the presenter. Forget the support you have in terms of presentation aids, technology, and even PowerPoint and the content on screen. This is all about you!

Firstly, find out why you have less than 30 seconds interacting with others before they have formed a solid opinion about you. And that those 30 seconds may well be nothing to do with your time on stage.

If the fact that you have less than 30 seconds in which to make an impression on those you will present to has alarmed or even scared you a little, the next chapter looks at fear itself: What it is, how it is deeply rooted in our evolution and the considerable influence it has over our presenting ability. Discover how you can channel your fear into being a positive aspect of your presenting as opposed to negatively limiting your ability. You'll also find out how you can instantly reduce or remove any feelings of fear just by altering your physiology. After exploring how fear manifests itself and providing you with the tools to manage it, we'll address the root causes of your fear and then contextualise them in a way that puts them into a much less destructive manifestation.

In the next chapter, we'll introduce readers to one of the most amazing breakthroughs in modern psychology – mirror neurons. We'll explain what they are and how they can help you learn from other great presenters giving fantastic presentations with little or no conscious effort at all. How cool is that?

Another powerful ally or enemy to you as a Power Presenter relates to a mental activity known as anchoring. We'll explain what anchors are and how they get hard-wired into the human psyche. We will also let you know why anchors can be both positive and negative in terms of how they affect all of us, their 'owners', while we're being presenters. Finally on this topic, discover how to anchor a positive state so that you are able to 'enter' that state as easily as pressing a light switch.

Moving outside your Power Presenter's head, the next chapter offers advice on dress code starting with answering the question: What should you wear when presenting to an audience? Discover tricks you can employ to help make you more distinctive and memorable (in a professional sense) to others so that they are more likely to remember you and actively seek you out after you have finished your presentation.

By reading the section on body language you'll realise that how you look and move while presenting often communicates more than what's coming out of your mouth or even than what's on the screen next to you.

That chapter also offers a number of best practice dos and don'ts. Discover how you can literally 'own the stage' and how you can actively manage audience attention and engagement levels using your own body language. You'll also learn more about how you can 'read' the audience and how to judge their engagement towards different aspects of your presentation so that you can adjust your delivery accordingly.

As well as looking at body language, there is also a chapter on actual language. How you talk to the audience directly influences their engagement and uptake of what you are talking about. We'll challenge you as a Power Presenter to think about your message in relation to how the audience will receive it and 'what's in it for them'. This chapter offers advice on how to direct your message in a language that is both relevant and pertinent to the audience itself more than talking how you would to yourself.

Another aspect of language that is important to professional communicators involves representational systems; these are the systems we access, process and store information in once it is received through any of the five senses. In addition to the specific words and phrases we use, you'll discover how to increase your levels of rapport (and therefore influence) with the audience through identifying and utilising their representational system preferences. This in turn will help you build the effectiveness of your presentations by communicating to a full range of representational systems in your presenting language.

In the final chapter of this section we will illustrate the importance of you being able to set the tone, pitch and styling of your presentation, coupled with your overall appearance to reflect the mood of the audience, and the core message or messages of the presentation.

In summary, the first section is all about maximising the impact and effectiveness of you as a presenter. After all, if the presenter didn't add anything to the event then it might as well have been an email! You as a Power Presenter are vitally important to almost any presentation event. You are the living link between the audience and the subject matter and those all-important key messages. It is your role to manage the audience and the key message relationships in order to optimise the communication from one to the other.

Incidentally, although you are encouraged to read the section from beginning to end, we recognise just how short of time most of us are in the 21st century. Therefore, the book has been designed so that you can also dip in and out of it at will. It may be that you need to address a particular aspect of your role as a presenter. If this is so, then simply look it up in the Contents and treat that chapter as a stand-alone training module. While we're on the subject of time, let's move on to look at the moment in time when your presentation starts.

Understand when your presentation starts

"The way to develop decisiveness is to start right where you are, with the very next question you face."
Napoleon Hill

In this first chapter, let's broaden out the presentation beyond those precious minutes when you are delivering your key messages from the stage. Because, did you know that your persona (the perception the audience has of you) directly influences their level of engagement with the presentation? To the majority of presenters, their presentation begins the moment they stand on stage and either say their first word or when their introduction screen appears. Well, here's another opportunity to significantly improve your presentation skills by doing… very little really.

To begin with, turn the tables metaphorically and identify the window of opportunity that your audience has to present themselves to you because, in actual fact, your presentation should start when you and your audience first meet (on the day of the presentation) and end when you go your separate ways (again, that day). Suddenly that finite window of time often becomes much longer. Furthermore, it goes from an intense number of actual presentation minutes to the longer, more relaxed period of time that happens to contain the said presentation minutes.

If you are the first speaker of the day, or after a refreshment break, you can utilise the time before you present to interact with members of the audience. This lets you identify a couple of people's names (who you can impressively refer to during your main presentation). Also, you can judge the general mood of the gathering over a relaxed coffee or text and email break. Another trick you can employ is to canvas audience opinion of any previous presentations, to discover the sort of thing that is liked and disliked by that gathering.

There are other forms of presentation too that can be stretched over a longer period of time. Consider the typical sales pitch or company credentials presentation. More often than not the presenter is led to a room, given a few minutes to set up and connect their laptop to the projector and speakers etc. What often happens is a period of irrelevant small talk both during set up and take down. These are both terrific opportunities for the presenter to prime the audience and canvas their objectives for the presentation (during set up) and deal with any unanswered questions or objections (during take down). In this scenario, imagine both periods as slide-less slides. They should be equally crafted into the overall presentation, even scripted if necessary. Pull together a list of the really important things you'd like to know before the core presentation and also a list of things to wrap up after it has finished. Now you can use each list as an *aide-mémoire* to make sure that you maximise the entire window of opportunity.

Here's a thought-provoking couple of statistics. Firstly, psychologists, writers and seminar leaders caution that you only have 7 to 17 seconds of interacting with strangers before they form an opinion of you, says David Saxby, president of Phoenix-based Measure-X, a company that specializes in helping utilities improve their customer service and sales. Worse though is that it takes them three times as long to change their minds about you. So that means that more often than not, the person or persons you are presenting to, particularly in business presentations such as credential or sales pitches, have formed an opinion and impression of you before Slide 1.

And here's another one from Iowa State University, College of Family and Consumer Sciences. Human beings have the capacity to take in an enormous amount of information when they first meet someone, and much of the information is visual appearance information. Human perceivers start to formulate and develop impressions within the first 30 seconds of meeting someone. Early information colours interpretation of future information. In other words, you don't lose your first impression, but build on it during future encounters, or the impending presentation.

So all of a sudden, the carefully timed 30-minute presentation is often only a part of a longer, overall encounter. In other words, as well as crafting your presentation and rehearsing it over and over again, you also need to include the following: Have you created your slide-less slides for use before and after the main event? What will the audience think of you when they first see you and is it the ideal? Have you identified the entire amount of time you have to get your messages across and do you have a plan outside your precious slide presentation?

In summary, go beyond your presentation and consider yourself part of it. The key to a good presentation is in part to present you appropriately. They say a picture is worth a thousand words, and so the 'picture' you first present says much about you to the audience you are meeting. Ask yourself whether your appearance is saying the right things to help create the right first impression.

Are you dressed appropriately? And anyway, what is the appropriate dress for the meeting or occasion? And what about your grooming? For the most part, clean and tidy appearance is appropriate for most business and social occasions. A good haircut or shave combined with clean and tidy clothes and neat and tidy make up. Overall, one of the best things you can do for your self-confidence amongst other things is to make sure your grooming is appropriate and helps make you feel the part, act the real deal and don't dream it, really be it!

Hopefully in this chapter we've highlighted that the typical presentation actually is longer than just delivering the carefully created deck of key messages. The presentation actually starts as soon as you and the audience come into direct contact with each other and doesn't end until you all go your separate ways after the event, seminar or whatever.

Consider that whenever you come into contact with all or some of your audience, you are in a way already on stage so go ahead and play your part. Remember that the audience will have formed opinions about you, often some time before you even stand up in front of them, and with this in mind think of yourself as an integral part of your presentation and that the whole event lasts for the entire time you and your audience are together on that occasion.

Well, wasn't that just what you wanted to hear? Now, instead of being scared to death about your minutes on stage, now you have to fear the entire event right from the get go? With that in mind, let's move onto a chapter all about one of the most potentially debilitating things almost any presenter has to face and deal with – Fear itself.

Processing & removing fears

"Courage is resistance to fear, mastery of fear, not absence of fear."
Mark Twain

To begin with, what is fear? To give a somewhat simplistic response, fear is one of six human primary emotions. As such it is deep rooted within our evolutionary hard-wiring and can influence our behaviour and how we feel much more than we are consciously able to control. So with that in mind, it is absolutely imperative that as a Power Presenter, you are able to understand, manage and channel your fears related to presenting in front of others.

At the most basic level, humans fear harm; that harm may be

physical or psychological. The harm people fear may be from physical pain or something psychologically based such as being afraid of losing a valued friendship. Human survival depends on developing techniques and strategies that result in the avoidance or escape from situations that cause physical or psychological pain. Presenting to others is one such example in many, many cases (well, so the presenters intently believe, anyway). In actual fact, research has shown that the fear of pain can often be more intense and miserable than experiencing the actual pain itself.

Importantly, fear is often experienced in advance of any potential harm, and so for the most part we have the opportunity of recognising and addressing our fears before they have the chance to take control of our behaviour on stage. As a consequence, many typical PowerPoint presenters will literally invent a story to justify their fear and so avoid having to take action and to address it head on. Well, that doesn't really help, does it?

Fear is made up of three different 'forces' and they are as follows:

1. Physiology – How the human body is used in terms of posture, breathing, movement, etc.

2. Focus – Whatever a person mentally focuses on, will result in them feeling that way.

3. Language & meaning – The way you verbalise an experience determines the way you feel about it because it influences the meaning in your own mind.

What you need to do is turn your own fear of presenting into a more positive form of energy, and you can do so by addressing each of these three forces individually. Here are the tools to help you.

Firstly, let's look at how you can refine and manage your own physiology. Begin by recognising what a person looks like when they are fearful and identify differences between them and those who simply ooze confidence. Notice the typical signs that communicate fear. When you look at their bodies, fearful people will exhibit tense muscles, shallow breathing, stilted movements, and sometimes a nervous laughter. When you look at the faces of fearful people, their eyebrows may well be raised and straightened, their mouth slightly open and lips tense (small) and drawn back

Take a look at TV programmes such as *Dragon's Den* and you'll see fear in many of the contestants pitching for the investment of the dragons. It's a good idea to make a list of the things that signal a person is fearful. This helps you recognise the factors more easily and more efficiently commit them to memory. As well as making a list of the factors that indicate somebody is fearful, study confident people and compare their individual actions with what's on your list.

Now, using a mirror or a partner, adopt a fearful posture and then switch to feeling confident, now switch back again. Spend a few minutes moving between these two states so that you can turn each on and off like a switch.

Here's a really powerful tool you can use to channel your own fear (and it's scientifically proven). Fifty-five per cent of what governs how we feel (fearful or confident) is based solely on our posture and physiology. So any time you sense a feeling of fear, simply adopt your now learnt confident physiology. Fear gone or greatly reduced in an instant. It really is that simple to change how you feel!

The second aspect of managing your own fear is to have the ability to shift your focus. When you think of standing up and presenting and you start to feel that feeling of fear, what is your focus? Take time either alone or with others to think about and list all the things you are focussing on when thinking of presenting to others; be sure to think it through. If you are thinking 'all those people' why is that your focus and what is it about them that frightens you? Here's a formula you can use to understand your own fear-related focus:

What are you focussing on?

Why, then why is that why, finally why really are you focussing on that?

What exactly is the focus?

What exactly are you afraid of?

Why, then why is that why, finally why really are you afraid of that?

By now, you'll begin to uncover the root causes of your fear by understanding it in relation to what you are focussing on and the real reasons why. Now all you need to do is refocus and the fear will diminish. For example, if the root cause of your fear is a sense of impending embarrassment by forgetting your lines, fluffing your message and generally going wrong on stage, then let's give you a new focus.

Imagine yourself leaving the stage to a standing ovation. People are patting you on the back and coming up to shake your hand. For this to be effective, you need to really develop this mental image within your own mind. You can do this by adding detail and making your internal mental representation, big, bold and in colour. The sounds are loud and clear and you can even smell the room, and feel the steps of the stage under your feet. Please now close your eyes and spend five minutes developing and clarifying your internal movie. Once you have this clearly in your head, relax and open your eyes.

Whenever you start to sense fear about an impending presentation, play your movie and focus on all the detail as much as possible. You'll be astonished at how your feeling will change... once again, in an instant.

The third and final step for removing your sense of fear comes from a simple technique of changing how you internally communicate with yourself in relation to what is making you fearful. On a sheet of paper, or preferably on a computer screen, write a page or so describing how you are feeling towards an upcoming presentation and how you think it will go. Write down what you think will be good and what bad, make notes of the individual things that you think will or might happen and your thoughts and opinions of them. Now, read through what you have written and highlight every word and phrase that is negative (can't, won't, fail, miss, lose, etc.). In other words, pick out every time you associate something negatively with your presentation. As a separate exercise, do the same, but this time highlight every word and phrase that is positive (will, can, win, success, etc.). How many of each do you have? Typically, the more the percentage is negative, then the more fear you are associating with the event.

The final stage of this exercise is to replace all of your negativity with positivity. Literally, cross out every negative reference and replace it with a positive alternative and write a nice new pristine version with no negative references. Now, as regularly as you can, read to yourself your new entirely positive thoughts about your upcoming presentation and, lo and behold, that's what your brain will provide you with.

In summary, whenever you start to sense any fear related to presenting, firstly adopt your confident posture and physiology. Secondly, play your internal success movie and make sure to focus on the sensory detail. Thirdly and finally, read your positive presentation commentary. Handling fear is a lot to deal with the way you mentally process and, with that in mind, the next chapter explores an aspect of psychology that can revolutionise the way you learn to present in future. What we're talking about are mirror neurons; in our opinion, one of the greatest presenter-related discoveries of the 20th century.

Mirror neurons – Look at the best, learn to be the best

"The brain is like a muscle. When it is in use we feel good. Understanding is joyous."
Carl Sagan

Within this next chapter, we'll look at how you, the Power Presenter, can not only learn from other great presenters giving fantastic presentations, but also how you can do so in a very short space of time and with little or no real effort (sounds promising huh?). What we're going to reveal is an undeniable shortcut to presenting excellence. And although a lot of great presenting is learnt from practice, practice and more practice, this invaluable mental asset that we all possess is there, available for you right now.

If it's a mental asset, then it must be to do with the brain, right? Yes absolutely, and although there are many parts of the brain that you can fine tune (many covered in this book) to improve your presenting, this next one is one of the most beneficial and easiest to deploy.

Firstly, we need to go deep into the brain and to look at precisely how it works. Our brains consist of around 100 billion neurons, which are the basic information processing structures within our heads. They are connected to each other by synapses through which information flows from one neuron to another. Information passes between neurons by way of tiny chemical reactions in each cell that then send an impulse (electrical or chemical) along the synapse to the next neuron. The process of a neuron sending an impulse out is referred to as firing. So in summary, the human brain functions by way of neurons sending signals to other neurons (millions and millions of them) using synapses as connectors.

While there are as many as 10,000 specific types of neurons in the human brain, generally speaking, there are just three different kinds: motor neurons (that convey motor information), sensory neurons (that convey sensory information) and inter-neurons (these act as middlemen between other neurons, receiving information from the body's outside or inside environment and passing it along to the brain for further processing).

There's a particular type of neuron that's only recently been discovered by Italian neuroscientist Giacomo Rizzolatti known as a 'mirror neuron'. A mirror neuron is one that fires (sends or receives impulses) both when an animal or person acts and when that being observes the same action being performed by another. Thus, the neuron 'mirrors' the behaviour of the other, as though the observer were itself acting. In other words, we learn and hard-wire our brains partly by copying the actions of others, and by doing so develop and embed new neural pathways.

It is believed that mirror neurons developed in the brain to speed up learning in both animals and humans; they reduced the evolutionary time needed to survive and so made that aim significantly more likely.

Mirror neurons can often be the cause of such bad habits as nail biting and hair chewing. So in the case of nail biting, for example, it can become a habit as a result of seeing others do it and then copying them (sub-consciously). Over time it becomes hard-wired by creating its own established neural pathway and the longer it continues to be a habit, the more established and harder it is to break. However, it is possible to break habits and once you know the theory, the practice becomes somewhat easier.

Incidentally, if you want to break a habit, it is necessary to 'rewire' or break an established and embedded neural pathway, by wiring in a new set of activities. A good analogy is that of a vinyl record (for those of you who are old enough to remember such things). Imagine the needle or stylus repeatedly staying in the same continuous groove and playing the music in the same order time after time – that's the habit. Now if a large scratch is made across the surface of the record, the stylus will jump out of its groove and play some parts of the tune in a different order – that's the habit broken. Mentally, when you realise you are doing something as a bad habit, make a dramatic behavioural change (scratch your own record) and you'll start to disrupt that habitual activity.

So how is it that the cause of bad habits can be an asset to you as a Power Presenter? To explain simplistically, mirror neurons can also fire and so create presenting-related neural pathways that are beneficial to you, the presenter. What's even better is the fact that you can learn to be a Power Presenter by simply watching and listening to other good presenters. What you need to do is get hold of some examples of good presenters giving great presentations. These may be in the form of attending conferences and seminars, obtaining training DVDs, or straight from the TV. Another particularly good source of excellent presenting skills is *YouTube*.

As you sit and watch another (good) presenter, imagine that it is you up there on the stage. And as you do, start to become aware of how you are feeling. Notice how your physiology is becoming more upright, proud and in actual fact that of a person exuding confidence. And as you go through this process, and you can do so as often as you like, you'll be actually training your own brain to work and in some ways think like that of an excellent presenter. If this sounds too good to be true, let me offer a couple of supporting examples of how your brain mirrors the behaviour of others. Firstly, for those of you who drive a car, I'm sure you'll all have been a passenger at some time or other and when you were, I'll bet you can recall instances when your own feet momentarily moved towards some invisible brake pedal? For those of you who are soccer fans, how many times have you been sat in front of the TV watching a match and as the intensity of the game develops, you found your own feet twitching as you tried to help a player in your team get to the ball before the opponent does? Those are just a couple of examples of mirror neurons doing what they do best; copying the actions of others.

In this section we've covered both the benefits and negative aspects of mirror neurons, so it's worth reiterating that, yes, you can become a better Power Presenter by watching and letting your brain mirror the actions of other good presenters, but you can also run the risk of becoming a worse presenter by sitting through too many bad and mind-numbingly dull PowerPoint presentations. So really it's a case of surrounding yourself with good presenters whenever possible and avoiding too many of those bullet point laden lists that we all have seen far too many of.

In the next chapter, we're going to look at another aspect of how our brains function. This time, we're talking about how you can lock in a positive mindset or group of behaviours and we'll give you the tools to help illuminate those annoying negative aspects of how you feel like you do. What we are referring to is the subject of anchors, or triggers that lead to a set of behaviours, a certain mindset or both.

Anchors, anchoring and firing

"As long as habit and routine dictate the pattern of living, new dimensions of the soul will not emerge."
Henry van Dyke

Anchors are both a great and potentially disastrous psychological aspect of humans that can both help and hinder us as presenters. In this next chapter, we will explain what anchors are and how they get hard-wired into the human psyche. We'll also let you know why anchors can be both positive and negative in terms of how they affect their 'owner'.

You'll then discover how to anchor a positive state so that you are then able to 'enter' that state as easily as clicking on a light switch. You'll also discover how to collapse any limiting or damaging negative anchors equally and straightforwardly.

To begin with, let's explain what an anchor is (in psychological terms). Anchoring is reminiscent of Pavlov's experiments with dogs. Pavlov sounded a bell as the animal was given food. The animals salivated when they saw the food. After some pairings of the bell and the food, the bell alone elicited salivation.

Anchors are stimuli that literally alter your state of mind; what you are thinking and how you feel. For example, imagine being at the funeral of a loved one and at a time when you are feeling morose and extremely sad, the other attendees often pat you on the back and console you regarding your loss. What they are actually doing is creating a trigger that in future will illicit those negative feelings as soon as somebody touches your back in a similar way.

Some anchors are entirely involuntary. So the smell of a cake baking in the oven may take you back to your childhood. Hearing a particular song may remind you of a certain person or event in your life. These anchors work automatically and you may not be aware of the triggers.

Establishing an anchor means producing the stimuli (the anchor) when the resourceful state is experienced so that the resourceful state is hard-wired to the anchor. For example, the act of touching your left elbow may be wired as the trigger for a particular positive state

In the next stage of the process, we'll explain how you can literally anchor those feelings (the positive ones). Finally, you'll receive the tools you need to also be able to remove or collapse any harmful or limiting negative anchors.

The aim of this is to provide you with yet another psychologically tried and tested technique for improving how you feel and, ergo, how you present on stage.

To start with, we'd like you to think of times when you felt superbly positive and then note down in detail what that feeling feels like.

Spend some time doing this and pay particular attention to your physiology, heart rate, breathing and even such small details as sweaty palms and how often you blink. After completing this part of the exercise, you should recognise, or are at least more aware of, what physical components make up a positive feeling. What we now need to do is to create a shortcut so that you can press a button and feel this way whenever you want to.

Whenever you need to feel a particular way, such as oozing confidence as you walk towards the stage to deliver your keynote presentation, all you need to do is as follows:

1. Decide on the state you want to anchor or how you want to feel. For example, being super confident.

2. Choose an anchor (or switch) that you'll use to trigger the resourceful state in an instant. For example, touching your left elbow three times.

3. Build the mental representation in your mind so that you begin to really experience the state. Now go through your five senses and add the detail of each so that you greatly intensify how you feel. You need to make your mental representation really bright and vivid, loud, proud and intense in every sense (literally).

4. When the experience is truly as intense as you can make it, and you are really in the desired state, attach the anchor (for example, touch your elbow three times).

5. Now do something else to change how you feel, such as breathing deeply and starting to relax.

6. Repeat the steps (3 to 5) several times, each time making the memory more intense. This is now helping to hard-wire the anchor and more importantly attaching the anchor to that intense feeling.

7. Now return to a mentally neutral state and then apply the anchor and check that the required state occurs.

8. The more times you practise steps 3 to 5, the more powerful the anchor will become.

As we've already established, anchors are powerful in terms of how they can trigger a specific set of feelings and physiology. Unfortunately, they can work both positively and negatively. What we need to be able to do now is to remove, or at least reduce, the effect of negative anchors. Firstly you need to recognize the negative anchors that are within you and have been hard-wired over your lifetime. Think of times when you felt overly negative; but this time, note down in detail what that feeling feels like. Now you should recognise, or be at least more aware of what components make up a negative feeling.

So let's go ahead and reduce the significance of a negative anchor. Begin by really mentally concentrating on one of your own personal negative anchors and, once you have a clear mental representation of it, do the following: Firstly, remove any colour and make the image of it black and white in your head. Now, with regard to any sounds that are part of your representation, make them completely incongruous. If there are voices, make them sound like cartoon characters; turn low, threatening tones into high squeaky noises. If there are smells and aromas associated with your negative mental representation, remove them or alter them to something much nicer. Finally, if there are any tactile sensations (and there almost certainly will be) literately dilute them so you can hardly feel them.

Now take this combined mental representation and put the little tiny thing into your hand (almost invisible as you look, feel and listen to it); the hand you use to fire your positive anchor. In our example, it was the right hand touching the left elbow.

Here comes the clever bit; now fire your positive anchor by squashing your insignificant negative anchor between your right hand and left elbow. Notice how the positive one is far stronger and how you now feel positive. Every time you are experiencing any anchor-based negativity, repeat this exercise.

Just as this exercise is aimed at improving your presentation from the inside, here's a way to smarten things up externally. In the next chapter, we're going to look at aspects related to your dress code; what your attire says to the audience (and you) about yourself.

Dress code – Be respected and remembered

"Clothes make the man. Naked people have little or no influence on society." Mark Twain

So just what should you wear when presenting to an audience? The question in itself presents a plethora of thoughts and ideas relating to presentation content type, audience demographics and many other considerations. In addition to this, our experience and skill set are honed around helping presenters present more effectively as opposed to being anything to do with fashion, dress sense and style (in this respect).

So when we refer to dress code, we are talking more about attention to detail and some ways to use what you wear to your advantage as part of your presentation.

Let's start with what, to many, will be common sense and second nature – Footwear. What you wear on your feet says a lot about the sort of person you are. If you wear leather brogues, then you are thought to be professional and authoritative. However, if the brogues are scuffed or in need of a clean, you will be perceived by many as being uncaring, lacking attention to detail and even untrustworthy. Trainers can be worn to show you are athletic, a sort of hands-on individual or someone who is maybe creative and/or non-conformist. When planning to present give some consideration to what you will wear on your feet and how that will influence the audience's perceptions of you and your key messages.

Another dress aspect to consider is the jacket. Should you wear one or should you be more of a roll up the sleeves and get stuck in sort of guy (or gal)? This is a technique employed by many politicians; to indicate that they mean action and are 'can do' types. When deciding whether or not to wear a jacket, consider what the audience are doing and decide whether you want to appear as one of them, one who wants to be respected by them or one of the aforementioned 'can do' individuals. Along with the shoes, your choice relating to a jacket can alter the way an audience perceives what you are presenting.

It's worth also mentioning the simple tie (for men), which incidentally is currently out of favour in a lot of business situations. We have no research or expertise to offer regarding whether to wear a tie or not and how it alters audience perceptions. However, there was a degree of outrage when BBC news anchors removed their ties and, now that all the dust has settled so to speak, the anchors have gone back to wearing ties (however, not all field reporters do). What we do know is that the way you wear your tie says something about you. Firstly, for the absolute correct way to wear your tie, the top of the 'v' or point at the (wide) end should be level with the top of your belt. Too short and you risk losing authority visually, too long and you are a hippie! Then there is the tie knot. A search of the Internet will reveal how to correctly tie a tie knot and how not to, but in our experience, the smaller the knot, the less professional the presenter. But too big can also reduce credibility. As we said, the Internet is probably the best way to learn more about this specific aspect of dress.

It goes without saying that both male and female presenters should wear clean clothes that are in good condition and this is more important than the particular style and fashion of the garments.

Here's a little bit of advice for those that present at conferences and events that run over a number of days: Dress the same every day;

this doesn't mean wearing the exact same shirt every day but the shirts should be identical. This way the audience and delegates will recognise you each day. Notice that on many TV dramas and sitcoms, the characters always wear the same overcoat or the same jumper. It all helps the audience recognise and relate to the character. Obviously, if for some reason you want to not stand out in the coffee breaks, then change how you dress only for the presentation itself; if you've announced some bad news such as job losses for example.

If you present regularly, you may want to develop and mould your dress code as part of your overall presentation personality. Again, if you look on TV there are personalities who always have aspects of their dress that are instantly recognisable, such as the banking expert wearing bright red braces or the personality chefs who are never out of their kitchen smocks (even though they are in a studio with no likelihood of doing any cooking). This incidentally leads on to the subject of dressing up. By this we mean dressing in a way that communicates that you are dressed to undertake some specific type of activity such as wearing a tracksuit; an act that says that you are about to indulge in something sport related.

You can enhance your own presentation personality by identifying what it is best to wear both in terms of what it says about the sort of person you are and how it relates to the subject matter – Leather elbow pads sewn onto suit jackets communicates school teacher!

One final point on the matter of dress code that must be made relates to personal hygiene. Very often, presenters are nervous and tend to perspire. This is often compounded by hot stage lighting. The message is simple; never ever wear clothes that show when you are perspiring (such as dark blue shirts for men) and deodorants should be used too. If, for some reason, you are one of those who won't deodorise or use an antiperspirant, then dress accordingly (avoiding the blue shirt for example).

In summary, as a Power Presenter, part of your presentation relates to how you look. This aspect should be considered in as detailed a way as the actual content of the presentation itself. After all, even before you've uttered a single word or presented any screen content, you will have come into the view of the audience and they will have made their initial impressions about you. They will have in fact already made a judgement about your presentation even before you start it. So aim for that judgment to be as positive and beneficial to the content and key messages as possible.

Whatever clothing you decide is right for you, under it is a body and that body has ways and means of communicating all by itself. In the next chapter we're going to describe how you can better manage your own body language and be able to start to read what is being communicated by others.

Body Language – An introduction to the subject

"The most important thing in communication is hearing what isn't said."
Peter Drucker

In this chapter, we'll look at an often overlooked but nevertheless important aspect of both the presenter and presenting – Body language. To quantify the importance of body language, Albert Mehrabian (UCLA Professor and author of *Non-Verbal Communication*) quantified that when referring to attitudes and feelings, i.e. talking emotionally, a mere 7% of human-to-human communications are represented by the words actually spoken. A further 38% is communicated via tone of voice and a massive 55% is transmitted (ergo, and received) through non-verbal communication, a large proportion of which is made up of body language.

So what is body language? A search on *Google* will reveal that there are literally thousands of books on what has become a well respected and relatively advanced science. Our aim here is somewhat simpler in that we would like to share sufficient information relating to presenting without overloading you with irrelevance. In answer to the question of what body language is, *Wikipedia* states: *Body language is a form of non-verbal communication, which consists of body posture, gestures, facial expressions, and eye movements. Humans send and interpret such signals almost entirely subconsciously.* In other words and from a presenting perspective, how you look and move while presenting communicates often more than what's coming out of your mouth or even than what's on the screen next to you. What's more, the audience also silently communicate a great deal relating to how they feel about what you are communicating to them.

The use of body language offers you the opportunity of greatly emphasizing parts of your presentation. So fundamentally, if you are stood or sat rigidly behind a lectern or desk, then most of your body is hidden – opportunity missed.

So what do you want to communicate when on stage in front of your audience? Here are a number of best practice dos and don'ts to follow: Cues such as covering your mouth when talking and avoiding eye contact with the audience may suggest that you are being less than truthful and so should be avoided when making key points. This also implies that you need to look away from the presentation screen too, and that's often another comfort blanket ripped from under your feet. As well as making eye contact with the audience and not covering you mouth, showing the palms of your hands (specifically your exposed wrists) indicates a degree of truthfulness and openness.

With regard to overall appearance, remember that how you appear is how you feel. So if you stand motionless, round shouldered, breathing in a shallow fashion and looking down, metaphorically hoping that the stage would open up and swallow you, then guess what? It's highly likely that you'll be experiencing a considerable amount of fear. Conversely, if you stand there and push your chest out, look out into the auditorium and hold your head high, then you'll feel how you look – Confident! The same is true when looking at how a presenter moves around on stage. A common term used is that somebody 'owns the stage' and that's again an effective standpoint for the Power Presenter to take. So what is meant by 'owning the stage'? In essence it is literally yours; all of it. So don't stand motionless in a corner of it. Stride around using as much of it as you can and take the opportunity of looking at different areas of your audience. Learn to appear as if you are engaging with different sections of the audience at different times as you present.

Another aspect of body language to consider relates to the fact that often the stage puts the presenter physically above (higher up) the audience and so they are literally talking down to them. This is all well and good if you want to come across as being authoritative and an expert on the topic of your presentation. However, there are some messages that require a different, more sensitive approach when communicating them. If you want to appear part of the same team as the audience, if you want them to feel they are your equals or if you are praising them or rewarding them then it's often wise to communicate at their level. Here that means not looking down on them. If you find yourself having to give these types of message, we suggest you might want to literally sit on the edge of the stage (or on a chair). Alternatively, why not leave the stage altogether and go and stand with the audience while looking back at the screen, as they do. Providing you haven't had to leave the microphone, then you can communicate very sensitively from this position and the audience will be duly appreciative.

As a Power Presenter, it's not only your own body language you need to be aware of. What the audience are communicating back to you by way of non-verbal feedback is also very important to acknowledge and respond to. For example, if they start to fidget, chances are you've been presenting for too long and it's time for a break. Alternatively, they are simply bored!

Become aware of where the audience is directing their attention and if you start to lose them then make attempts to re-engage them with your presentation. If there are only a minority of the audience looking directly at you or the screen then that's an indication that others have lost interest. You may need to move on to the next point, bring your presentation to an end or introduce a break.

Research has identified that humans have a relatively short attention span when receiving information. Typically, they can handle 20 minutes at a time before they need a soft break. This may be as 'soft' as just breaking their concentration with an anecdote or a couple of questions and answers. Another effective soft break is to ask the audience to just stand up and shake themselves down. What this entails is getting them to stand and shake their arms and legs for a few seconds just to get the blood flowing again. As a best practice guide, people can only effectively absorb information for one hour (including two soft breaks) before needing a hard break. This means toilet, refreshment and text message opportunities. In other words, doing something completely different for a few minutes.

These timings are very much a guide and there may well be times when your audience is fully engaged and you can therefore keep going. The key is to be able to recognise and respond to their body language over and above being aware of your own physiological performance.

In summary, your body language says a lot to your audience and it primes your brain as to how you feel at that moment. Therefore it's important to develop your non-verbal communication skills if only insomuch as it will help with your self-confidence on stage. So recognise and refine what you communicate non-verbally both to the audience and yourself. In addition, make sure you are aware of and respond to what the audience is communicating back to you.

Although Albert Mehrabian quantified that the spoken word can represent as little as 7% of what a person communicates, it does often account for a whole lot more. Therefore, in this next chapter, we'll discuss the aspect of communication that is comprised of what you say.

Language – It's about you, not me

"If you talk to a man in a language he understands, that goes to his head. If you talk to him in his language that goes to his heart."
Nelson Mandela

In this next section, we'll look at a simple but important aspect of the language of an engaging presentation. In other words, what is the best way to get the audience to really engage with what you are Power Presenting, purely from a language perspective? Let us begin by defining what we mean by engaging. In this context, engagement means the extent to which an audience member has a meaningful experience when exposed to visual, auditory or other experiential information delivered via the presenter.

In essence, for the audience member to engage, they need to feel that it is relevant to them and, ergo, that you are presenting to them individually. The first way you can improve your audience member engagement is to simply refer to the benefits to them. For example, and to explain what comes from classic sales training when presenting benefits, the presenter is much better to talk about the benefits to you (the audience) as opposed to how I'll deliver them (me being the presenter).

Evolutionarily, we are all hard-wired to be primarily concerned with looking after ourselves (number 1). So anything that is to do with us individually, we are more likely to engage with.

While on the subject of selling (as that is what many presenters are actually doing, selling their company, their message, themselves, and the like), consider this well known fact: When the audience is considering what they are being presented with, they will be evaluating a number of different factors. The first decision is about you, the presenter; the second is about your credibility; the third is about your message and the fourth is about relevance. These factors are often considered in this exact, precise, psychological order when you are presenting. However, there is a big difference between someone buying something from you and you selling them something.

The professional salesperson makes it extremely easy for their customers to buy because they know how to sell. Everyone loves to buy; no one wants to be sold. A great weakness of many salespeople is that they are product-centred and not people oriented. Therefore their comfort level is often reached and relied on by talking about their fantastic products or services. As a Power Presenter, think about your message in relation to how the audience will receive it and 'what's in it for them'. You may know everything there is to know about your presentation subject, but pay careful attention to how much it is best to share. If the aim of the presentation is to demonstrate that you the presenter are indeed a leading expert on your chosen subject, then fine, but in our experience, this isn't the real objective of many presentations. Yes, it's fine to build your credibility early on (a couple of slides, typically) but then, once built, move on and make your content what the audience is really interested in and engage them by directing your messages to them.

Even at the storyboarding stage of your presentation, make notes of each of the key messages you want to convey and then add how and why that's relevant to the audience. If you can't do the second step here, then question the first.

To summarise here, endeavour to make your presentation audience-oriented and not too self-focussed. Then direct your message in a language that is both relevant and pertinent to the audience itself. Finally, when rehearsing your presentation and indeed delivering it, make sure the focus is on you, you, you (the audience) and not to me, me, me (the presenter).

There is another clever aspect of spoken language that, once you understand and adopt, results in you being able to create rapport with more of your audience, more quickly and meaningfully. In this next chapter, we're going to talk about representational systems; the language each of us uses internally to process what we are hearing somebody else say.

Language – Representational systems

"Your purpose is to make your audience see what you saw, hear what you heard, feel what you felt."
Dale Carnegie

When thinking of communicating your messages to your audience, it is important to understand something about how we as humans internally communicate with ourselves. We use what are termed 'representational systems'. These systems are used to process information via or through the senses. So, if a person is talking to oneself, and even if no words are emitted, they are communicating internally using their auditory representational system. If a person makes pictures in their head when thinking or dreaming, they are using their visual representational system. Another may be considering feelings in the body and emotions and this utilises the kinaesthetic representational system. These are the three main internal types of communication although gustatory (taste) and olfactory (smell) are also used but much less so. Visual (V), auditory (A), kinaesthetic (K), gustatory (G) and olfactory (O) are the five primary sensory modalities that humans use to experience the world around us. These modalities are also known as representational systems (rep systems) as they are the primary ways we represent, code, store and give meaning or language (linguistic) to our experiences.

Mostly as presenters, we work with just three of the representational systems: visual, auditory and kinaesthetic. Although the others are primary senses, gustatory and olfactory do not play a major role and can often be excluded from our communication language. However, there may still be a need for them in certain specific presentations such as when the subject matter is perfume or aftershave related. We each can access more than one representational system at the same time; listening to the radio, while looking at a picture of a loved one for example.

The key is that each person has a preferred representational system; some tend to be more visual, others auditory and some kinaesthetic. As a Power Presenter, you should try to use the language of all three so that they all can more easily process your message and content.

In another example provided by Roger Ellerton, PhD, ISP, CMC, Renewal Technologies Inc. (www.renewal.ca): When learning something new, some of us may prefer to see it or imagine it performed, others need to hear how to do it, others need to get a feeling for it, and yet others have to make sense of it. In general, one system is not better than another. However, depending on the context, one or more of the representational systems may be more effective: landscape painters, visual; musicians, auditory; athletes, kinaesthetic; and mathematicians, digital (digital refers to someone more cerebrally making sense of what they are hearing and as such isn't sensorially related). People at the top of their profession typically have the ability to use all of the representational systems and to choose the one most appropriate for the situation.

Depending on your preferred representational system(s), you may exhibit certain behaviours or characteristics. Before exploring these behaviours, please note that depending on what is going on in your life, or the context, you may change your preferred representational system(s). Hence, it is more useful to notice the representational system a person is currently favouring, rather than pigeon-holing a person. As a Power Presenter, play safe and use all three of the main representational systems (V, A, and K).

The following are generalizations on the characteristics of people with a preference for visual, auditory, kinaesthetic or digital. Remember, with all generalizations, there are always exceptions.

Visual – People with a visual preference, will tend to:

- Be organized, neat and well-groomed. Why? Because they want to look good. And what do they expect from you? Yes, the same thing!

- Use visualization for memory and decision making – often getting insights about something.

- Be more imaginative and may have difficulty putting their ideas into words.

- Speak faster than the general population. Why? Because they have a picture(s) in their mind and if it is a moving picture, there is a lot to tell in so little time!

- Prefer in-person interactions – to see the other person and his/her reactions.

- Want to see or be shown concepts, ideas or how something is done.

- Want to see the big picture.

- May not remember what people have said and become confused if you give them too many verbal instructions. However, if you can draw a map or picture for them, then they can see what you are saying.

- Remember faces more easily than names.

- Be distracted by visual activity and less so by noise.

Auditory – People with an auditory tonal preference, will tend to:

- Be more aware of subtle changes in the tone of your voice and be more responsive to certain tones of voice.

- Perceive and represent sequences and are able to remember directions or instructions more easily.

- Learn by listening and asking questions.

- Enjoy discussions and prefer to communicate through spoken language rather than the written word.

- Talk through problems and like to have someone available to serve as a sounding board for their ideas.

- Need to be heard.

- Be easily distracted by noise.

Kinaesthetic – People with a kinaesthetic preference, will tend to:

- Speak slower than the general population. Why? Because they need time to get in touch with how they feel about the topic.

- Be more sensitive to their bodies and their feelings and respond to physical rewards and touching.

- Learn by doing, moving or touching.

- Dress and groom themselves more for comfort than how they look.

- Make decisions based on their feelings.

- Stand closer to other people than those with a visual preference – to feel the other person's energy, whereas the person with a visual preference will stand back to see more of the other person (body language, etc.).

Digital – Digital is devoid of the senses. People with a digital preference, will tend to:

- Have a need to make sense of the world, to figure things out, to understand.

- Learn by working things out in their mind.

- Not be spontaneous, as they like to think things through.

- Have logic play a key role in the decision process as do facts and figures.

- Memorize by steps, procedures, sequences.

This fourth (non-sensory) representational system is important as it is a key way many members of an audience will mentally process much of the factual information you are presenting.

In summary, you need to design your presentation to address each of the following: Firstly, it should communicate in three language types – visual, auditory and kinaesthetic. Secondly, the information must be presented so that all of the audience are able to process it digitally. Thirdly, you as a presenter will have a preferred representational system and should try not to make your presentation too appealing just to those with the same rep system as yourself. If you would like to learn more about this subject or would like to identify your own representational system, visit www.renewal.ca.

Most of us would agree that it is not only what we communicate that is important, but also how; and in this next section we'll explore the different tones and styles you can adopt to most appropriately use to effectively convey your key messages to the audience.

What mood do I need to portray?

"It all has to do with the presenter as director or captain of the ship; for it is he that sets the pace, the course and the mood."
Phillip Adcock

When presenting, you need to set the tone of the presentation at the correct level, for example distinguishing between a group of executives, managers or manual workers. In these cases the key message will convey a differentiated level of need-to-know knowledge. Likewise the tone, pitch and styling of your presentation, coupled with your overall appearance, needs to reflect the mood of the audience and the key message of the presentation.

There will be times when good news is to be disseminated to a workforce. In such circumstances an upbeat mood can be portrayed in both a tone and pitch sense and even a clothing sense. With regard to clothing, as we've already discussed, be aware of not becoming the message of your own presentation. If you are presenting to a collection of work colleagues who are familiar with you having an exuberant dress sense then maintaining this would be acceptable. However, presenting to an unknown group the dress sense may need to be reined in.

Just as a mental note, consider presenting the following events:

1. Excellent sales figures.

2. Poor sales figures.

3. New product launch to a workforce or reseller channel.

4. Announcement of redundancies.

5. Retirement presentation.

6. Announcement of a colleague's bereavement.

With each of these scenarios one presentation style does not fit all. Consideration needs to be given to all aspects of mood and tone.

As an example I was scheduled to perform training for the Volkswagen group at their offices in the UK. As I was arriving at their reception, which was designed as a car showroom, I was greeted by a one-way stream of workers arriving in the reception area. Enquiring about this I was told an announcement to all staff was taking place. The news was of a positive nature, a good sales performance. On this occasion workers were standing in an environment surrounded by their product, being told how good things were. That is an example of how a presentation can be ripped away from the projector and computer and yet still provides a powerful message.

In contrast, for a redundancy announcement the tonal quality of the presentation needs to play an important element within the presentation. A sympathetic voice is an essential under these circumstances. Think also of the size of the group the announcement is made in front off. Ideally everyone within the organisation needs to be told the redundancies at the same time. Therefore arrange a seating environment where the news can be announced; this will prevent gossip spreading amongst staff.

The announcement of a colleague's bereavement would be best announced from within the audience in a smaller group, rather than from behind a lectern. As with the redundancy scenario, tonal and dress sense needs to be sympathetic, with no exuberance.

From these examples, being a Power Presenter is more than just the presentation. For a successful presentation the mood that you portray carries an important message with regard to the overall message.

Section 1 – You as a presenter: Summary

"If today were the last day of my life, would I want to do what I am about to do today? And whenever the answer has been 'No' for too many days in a row, I know I need to change something."
Steve Jobs

Well here we are at the end of the section that covered you as a presenter. In it we learnt the importance of maximising not just your time on stage to convey your message, but also the down time – those periods such as coffee breaks where you can develop and communicate your persona. We discussed ways of optimising the non-presenting time as an active contributory factor to the conveying of your messages and content. Use the entire time you are in the company of others, not just the part when you are on stage in front of them.

Use interaction time before the presentation to canvas their expectations and after your main event deal with any unanswered questions or objections. Pull together a list of the really important things you'd like to know before the core presentation and also a list of things to wrap up after it has finished. Then use each list as an *aide-mémoire* to make sure that you maximise the entire window of opportunity. We also discussed making sure that first impressions count; what did the audience think of you when they first saw you and was it the ideal? Again, this comes down to attention to detail and the fact that the presentation itself is only a part of your overall 'public appearance'.

Next we looked at one of the most debilitating factors presenters have to deal with; namely their own fear. We explained how it is both possible and relatively easy to begin to manage your fear by simply adjusting your own physiology. In other words, walk the walk of a confident person and that's how you'll feel. Then we gave you a tried and tested formula for contextualising your fear. In other words, once you think through what you are afraid of, then more often than not the fear itself dissipates. The final tool to handle fear involved you creating a more positive presentation commentary and then mentalising it (focus on positives, not negatives).

In the next chapter, we introduced mirror neurons and explored just how easily you can start to become a Power Presenter just by watching other masters of the craft. It is believed that mirror neurons are in our brains simply to speed up our learning (originally so we could survive as a species). Now we know more about how they work, go ahead and teach them stuff; specifically stuff related to being a Power Presenter. As you start to use them while you watch other great presenters, be sure to involve your physiology as well as your brain; adopt the same posture as those you are learning from if you really want the mirror neurons to work as well as they can.

Still concentrating on aspects relating to the brain, we then looked at the subject of anchors and how you can anchor a positive state so that you are then able to 'enter' that state as easily as clicking on a light switch. We also discussed how to get rid of or 'collapse' any negative anchors that you may possess. We showed how to build a positive mental state and internal representation and how then to attach an anchor or switch to it so that you can enter that mental state any time you want to just by pressing the right switch. We also explained that by reducing the size, colour, noise etc. of a negative anchor in your own mind really can reduce its debilitating capability.

Moving away from the brain, we then discussed how your very appearance is part of what the audience will use to develop their perception of you and your content. So clean shoes and appropriate (for that event and type of content) dress sense are important considerations, even the length of your tie. We also looked at how you can dress to convey a certain personality trait, such as wearing a shirt with the sleeves rolled up as so many politicians tend to nowadays.

We then revealed that the words you say can account for just 7% of what your overall presence on stage communicates and that you should pay attention to your body language and that of the audience. Try not to lose eye contact with the audience, fold your arms or cover your mouth when talking, as all of these can be perceived as you trying to hide something or lying. Remember also that if you want to feel confident, then stand like a confident person would stand. Finally here, do you want to talk down to the audience or appear as one of them? Whichever you choose, you can use your position in relation to the audience to enhance this perspective.

When you are presenting, try to develop a feedback loop. In other words, watch the audience and learn to pick up signals as to how engaged they are with your patter.

Next we looked at the language you use and the fact that if you make the content all about the audience they will be more attentive towards it. You should also try to cover the different representational systems as you talk so as to engage more of the audience. Although naturally, you would talk mostly in your preferred representational system, endeavour to use descriptors from each of the three main representational systems (visual, auditory and kinaesthetic) as part of your speech.

We then explored the tone of a presentation and looked at how it needs to be appropriate for the type of content and audience. Being a Power Presenter is more than just delivering the presentation. For a successful presentation the mood that you portray carries an important message with regard to the overall message.

In summary, the first section was all about maximising your impact and effectiveness as not just a presenter, but as a Power Presenter. As we said before, if the presenter didn't add anything to the event, then it might as well have been an email! Your role as a Power Presenter is vitally important to almost any presentation event you are participating in. You are the living link between the audience and the subject matter and key messages. It is your responsibility to manage the audience and key message relationships in order to optimise the communication from one to the other.

In the next section, we'll move on to the subject of the presentation: The information, rhetoric, lies, hypotheses or inane ramblings that you share with the audience. Because, however effective you are as a presenter, plain common sense dictates that you also need something to actually communicate.

Section 2

Your presentation

Section 2 – Your presentation: Introduction

"When I am getting ready to reason with a man, I spend one-third of my time thinking about myself and what I am going to say and two-thirds about him."

Abraham Lincoln

In the following section of this book, we'll explore a number of aspects related to the presentation itself. To start with, let's clarify what we mean by presentation – a performance; something, such as a lecture or speech that is set forth for an audience. In other words, the presentation section of this book deals with aspects relating to the audience-facing aspects of an event.

The section begins by looking at how you can theme and tone your presentation to better match the type of content and information you are communicating. For example, witticisms and humour may be acceptable in a marketing-related presentation, more so than in an event related to paediatric surgery.

Then we move on to explain how it is a good idea to treat your presentation as a form of story and how it can be developed as such with a beginning, middle and end. In addition, it should emotionally connect with an audience in a way that takes them on an emotional journey, slide by slide. Following on from this is the matter of the presenter having a good understanding of the key messages they want to present before they start designing any slides. In too many presentations, the presenter loses the audience simply because they failed to have their key message (or number of messages) carefully laid out in a logical order. Instead they just have a mass of information in their possession that they are determined to 'get out there'.

The section goes on to explain that human brains are notoriously poor at remembering things (particularly in an educational context).

Therefore, it follows that the more you say/spray, the less the audience are likely to take on board. Identifying, and then effectively delivering your key messages, is absolutely key to anyone wishing to become a Power Presenter.

We then go on to look at how you can identify the key message or messages you want the presentation to answer; then building the entire deck round these key points. We take that process a stage further and provide a great starting point for anyone starting to design their next presentation, relating to what is the single most important message you want your audience to take on board. Once you recognise what the audience wants, you can use design and creativity to make your intentions align with their expectations.

After covering presentation key messages, we discuss some key time-related considerations that need to be covered to ensure a clear and concise presentation. How long is the presentation? How long should it be for you, the event and most importantly to be effectively absorbed by the audience? Once the time for the presentation has been decided, and how long the presentation is to be, we then explore how many slides to present during your allotted time.

As we've just mentioned, a key aspect of a good presentation is how much of it gets absorbed or mentally taken on board by the audience. As part of this, there is a section ahead that explains how we as humans actually remember things. We do this by looking at how our memories have developed and why they can be somewhat unreliable. In the case of the audience's presentation-receiving brains, both their short term and long term memories have responsibilities, and we go on to explain what each are.

The next chapter explores the design of different types of presentation, each created with the likely number in the audience being a consideration. For example, just the screen size and its distance from the audience will directly influence both how visible and impactive the contents are.

Going back to the subject of audience attention and how much they can really take on board, there is a chapter in this section that quantifies how long a presentation should be; not in terms of the amount of information that the presenter needs to communicate, but in relation to how much the audience can absorb. What we're talking about here is human attention span. There is a scientifically proven time span of 20 minutes that presenters should be mindful of and it is explained in this chapter.

Having talked about the tone and style you adopt so as to be in line with audience expectations, in this next chapter we focus on a specific aspect of how to alter how you present depending on who you are presenting to. If you are presenting to colleagues who know you well, then they already understand and recognise your personality. But, if you are new to your audience, then it is advisable to take a number of steps early in your presentation so as to create the suitable respect and rapport for the messages you are communicating. These are outlined in this part of Section 2.

Next we explore human communication (because that is what presenting is all about) and we take a metaphorical step back to consider how humans communicate with each other. The heart of the answer to this question lies in the fact that as a species we have evolved over many millions of years and that evolution has shaped how we communicate. This next chapter describes what evolution is and how it moulds and shapes much of our communication with each other. For example, did you know that visual images have been processed by human brains and their evolutionary predecessors for around 10,000 times as long as language and words have been around? So why is it that, in light of this evolutionary limitation, so much PowerPoint communication relies on words to communicate? We'll explain how and why it usually shouldn't.

Moving on to another deeply rooted aspect of human psychology, emotion, the book goes on to explain that it is impossible to escape the fact that as human beings, we are emotional. In fact, almost every decision that we make, we do so emotionally and not rationally. So as you sit in an audience absorbing a presentation, you are constantly filtering the contents, including how it is delivered, through your own emotions. Discover why understanding and working with the emotions of the audience is absolutely pivotal for all Power Presenters. For instance, from an evolutionary perspective, there are six key drivers that all humans are motivated by. We'll show you how you can tailor your presentation to meet each of these evolutionary drivers, with the result that you'll more effectively engage with your audience.

At this point, the book begins to focus more on the actual design of the structure of a presentation and begins by looking at the basic presentation cover slide (or Slide 1). We explore the full potential of the cover slide and offer advice as to how you and your audience can get more out of it and benefit from its existence. Next we demonstrate why there is a need for a template for making sure we pace the feed of information at an acceptable level, and that it depends on the type of audience.

In the next chapter we offer a step by step approach to managing data flow. For example, we show why you need to recognise and estimate the cognitive load threshold (a term explained in detail) of your audience and then feed the information to them at an acceptable level. We also discuss a presentation technique that is based on a psychological term known as 'cognitive dissonance', which is defined as a discomfort caused by holding conflicting cognitions (e.g. ideas, beliefs, values, emotional reactions) simultaneously. In terms of presenting, this relates to creating a managed form of audience confusion so that their attention is held and even increased.

In the following chapter, we further explain and quantify the very limited processing power of the human brain (particularly the short term memory related part, as discussed earlier). And here we provide the science behind it in terms of what 7±2 mental processing means in relation to presenting PowerPoint and how it necessitates slide building and the strict pacing of information imparting.

Next, we explore the matter of building slides. This relates to being able to build a slide to tell a story, as opposed to just going 'splat'; there it all is. Then we move on to animation, another well-established *PowerPointism*. Should, text, graphics, clips and images fade in, fly in, spin out, or whatever?

Like so many things related to presenting to an audience, the subject of presenting them with numeric data has a number of rules and guidelines which we summarise next. After that we move on to text, and offer recommendations relating to how we can create text-based slides that are more mentally manageable for an audience to comprehend and take on board. The book explains that the audience can read faster than you the presenter will be speaking and so why would you ever, ever want to put sentences on the screen (i.e. bullet points and the like) and then to read them out slowly and clearly.

While on the subject of words and numbers, you'll also discover that a presentation and a handout are very different things, with different uses and they shouldn't be combined.

In the next chapter, our aim is simple; to persuade readers just how inappropriate bullet points are in any presentation. We demonstrate using evidence and expert opinion, how bad and inappropriate those apparently innocuous, but so easy and convenient to use, bullet points are. Just as bullet points have mistakenly become an essential crutch for far too many PowerPoint presenters nowadays, so has the use of clip art. In the next chapter we explain the dos and don'ts of using these all too often used crass little cartoon images. We also go on to discuss the use of video, music and sounds and offer some scientifically-based best and worst practice.

Over and above words, numbers, video, music and text, the book then explores the often overlooked topic of whether the presenter is presenting their own presentation or one produced by somebody else. And why, when presented with someone else's presentation you need to make it your own.

So let's begin this section by looking at a good way to start the design of your presentation. Identify to yourself, what it is you are going to present, or in other words, what's the story you are going to tell your audience?

What is my story?

"Storytelling is not what I do for a living – it is how I do all that I do while I am living."
Donald Davis

In this brief section we'll take a look at how you can theme and tone your presentation to better match the type of content and information you are communicating. For example, witticisms and humour may be acceptable in a design-related presentation, more so than in an event related to advanced heart surgery.

Before you can decide on the tone and style of your presentation, you should spend time identifying a few basic aspects. Begin by identifying the single most important message you want to deliver. Then identify the type of audience you will be delivering it to: Professionals, adults, men or women, young or old. Once you have your key message and your audience profile, you can start to think about the tone and style you wish to adopt. Don't worry if you haven't completed a degree in media studies or graphic design, there is a much simpler way to create an effective presentation style for your story. Think of your message as a TV genre and then decide what sort of thing would appeal to the type of audience you have in mind? Perhaps you picture it in a serious news style in which case you can look at the colours, fonts and screen layout used by the *BBC* or *SKY News*.

Alternatively, you may want a more light-hearted style; more along the lines of *Have I Got News For You* or other comedy or game shows. If this is the case, again you can look at the way they present images on screen, the colours used for the set and the tone and language in which they communicate. You will have a significantly better presentation if you adopt a story and a style and tone that are based on something already proven.

In terms of the story itself, like all good tales it should have a beginning, middle and an end. In addition, it should emotionally connect with the audience in a way that takes them on an emotional journey slide by slide. So here, you can begin with planning out the best way to deliver your key messages. Should each be set up with an introduction to it and then deliver it as the payoff afterwards? It may be that the 'come straight out with the message and then substantiate it with information and evidence in your story afterwards' method is a more successful approach. Whatever you decide, think of the entire presentation as a TV series; a series of episodes or sub-stories that are visually and editorially connected. Link your sub-stories or episodes together by consistently using the same styles, colours and fonts.

A very effective presenter we know uses the title of each slide in a very ingenious way as a bedrock of their overall presentation story. What they do is to take all the slide titles in isolation, copy them and then paste them into a single word processing document. When they do so, they read out a phrase, sentence or even paragraph that in itself is the summary or the story. This presenter even creates this message and attaches it to the handouts he gives to his audiences.

The point we're making in this section is that there should be a logical flow to your presentation in terms of the order of topics covered and information conveyed. Often you'll witness a presentation that just doesn't flow, and on many occasions this is because the creator has copied and pasted sections from a number of presentations to make that one. As a Power Presenter, being able to convey information as a story that has a beginning, middle and end and that follows a specific and relevant style and tone is a great way of making the event more engaging and the content therefore more memorable.

When telling a story, it's also good to decide the tense and tone you are going to use. For example, if you want to appear as one of the team (with the audience), you can talk of 'us' and 'we' as you narrate. Alternatively, you may need to be more authoritative (like the managing director delivering a companywide rebuke); here talk of the business and them. Part of this also relates to the way you talk, the timbre of your voice. Do you need to narrate in an engaging inflective way or simply deliver the message (*à la* reading the news)?

When you create the draft style for your story, consider adding a bit of suspense to it so that you intrigue your audience. This will increase their attention levels and lead to your content being even more memorable.

As a final point regarding the story you are creating, make sure that it isn't too boring or uninteresting so that you lose your audience. You know what it's like when you are engrossed in a good book or film, and that's what your aim should be in connection with your presentation story. There is another benefit of creating a story, in that it helps the audience remember a series of events, almost like going on a journey and passing various points of interest. As long as your story is suitably logical in its construction, the audience will be able to recall the key messages in the right order. Also, the mention of the story will trigger each of the key messages too. You'll have, in effect, emotionally connected your messages to your audience by the use of an engaging story.

Next time you have to create a presentation, take time to frame the key messages in a story. Frame the points in a logical order and link them by continuing your tale in an orderly direction (with a little added intrigue and suspense). Try not to simply enhance your key messages and to think of them only as a list of things to say. Find ways to emotionally engage the audience with each of them and to link them all together. In fact, a widely-used memory technique works just like this; users of it mentally place a list of things they wish to remember along a route they are familiar with (around their house, their journey to work, etc.). Then, as they mentally travel the route, they recall the items and in the intended order too.

It sounds straightforward, but you'd be surprised just how many presenters fail to separate out their key points and messages from all the supporting information in their presentation. In this next chapter, we'll provide tools and techniques for helping you identify and duly emphasise the key messages in your presentation.

What message am I conveying?

"You have to tell a complete story and deliver a complete message in a very encapsulated form. It disciplines you to cut away extraneous information."
Dick Wolf

In all too many presentations, the presenter loses the audience because they disengage from the subject matter. This often occurs simply because the presenter has omitted to have a predetermined message (or number of messages) carefully laid out in a logical order. Instead they just have a mass of information in their possession that they are determined to 'get out there'.

The point we're making here is that the presenter needs to recognise and understand the message or messages that they wish to convey. Often, a presentation will contain just a headline message and a small number of additional points that are important to take to the audience.

Where the process often breaks down is that when creating the presentation, they forget to structure or even identify what the message is that they want or need to convey. They just simply get all they have and verbally and visually spray the audience with it.

Here are some ideas to help you identify your presentation message or messages. Firstly, who are the audience and what they expecting? If you are attending a conference, what is the theme of the conference? Also, what is the knowledge level of the audience? Once you have an idea of what your most suitable messages are, you can decide if you need to set them up or frame them with supporting data or information.

Another way to identify the main message you intend to communicate is to note down every fact that is in your presentation and then order them in terms of a logical flow and, more importantly, importance. Then you can sense-check that your headline messages are still in line with what you perceive the audience will want.

Those of you who are experienced at presenting may wish to engage with some audience members before the presentation to canvas what they most want to take from the presentation. Then at least you can verbally emphasise what it is they wanted.

The point here is that as you create, design and deliver presentations, you should have identified and have in mind a message or messages you are intent on conveying. This is a much more audience-focussed approach than just pulling together everything you have.

Human brains are notoriously poor at remembering things (particularly in an educational context). Therefore, it follows that the more you say/spray, the less they are likely to take on board. Research has identified that in typical presentations, as much of 90% of the content has been forgotten within 24 hours of the audience being presented with it. So bearing this in mind, much of what you present may be forgotten by the audience very quickly.

As a means of combating this human frailty, the least you can do is inspect your content so that you identify the main message or messages you want to convey. These are what you should aim to embed within the brains of the audience as a minimum.

In future, start to look at the presentations of others and try to identify what the key messages are and any order with which they are delivered. Often you'll discover that the things you remember aren't what the presenter intended.

By adopting a more structured process of message identification and delivery, you'll improve your presentation effectiveness considerably. An added benefit is that it's also often easier to create the entire deck/presentation/story once you know what the key points really are.

Now that you've identified what you are going to present, it's time to also consider what it is that the audience wants to see, hear and learn. In other words, you need to check that your content is aligned with audience expectations. In the next chapter we ask you to consider the needs of the audience over and above just concentrating on the messages you want to impart on them.

What is the question you are going to answer?

"No question is so difficult to answer as that to which the answer is obvious."
George Bernard Shaw

In the previous section, we looked at how you can identify the key message or messages you want the presentation to answer; then building the entire deck round these key points. Here we will take that process a stage further and provide a great starting point for anyone starting to design their next presentation.

Start by simply asking, what is the one question that the audience wants an answer to? Think about their perspective of the event. For example, why are they attending? Then consider what is most important to them. This should be the absolute least that you then design into your presentation. There's an old saying that says you can't please all of the people all of the time. But by adopting this approach of identifying and answering the main question your audience has, you have more chance of pleasing more of them.

There is often a considerable disconnection between what the presenter expects to deliver and what the audience expects to learn. The fact that in 21st century society, time is an asset that so many people just don't have enough of means that you need to respect the time the audience has invested in coming to your presentation. Therefore, the least you can do is meet their most fundamental expectation. Hopefully, by following the ideas and recommendations in this book, you'll deliver a lot, lot more than that!

So remember, whether you have a ten-slide keynote presentation or 100 slides of detailed output, make sure that it serves a purpose that is in line with audience expectations. A failure to consider and recognise what the audience wants at a basic level is a sure-fire way to designing an ineffective presentation.

Incidentally, once you recognise what the audience wants, you can use design and creativity to make your intentions align with their expectations. By this we mean that the audience may want to learn something and you may be intent on selling. All you have to do is make sure that your presentation meets both requirements. For example, you can be open and honest with many audiences and explain to them that you will both promote and inform. This way, they'll more agreeably sit through your self-promotion in the knowledge that there is information to come (rewarding their time investment). In actual fact, in this scenario it is possible to combine information and promotion in the shape of what is termed the 'educative sell'; provide the information and then link how your product or service benefits them as a direct result.

Your presentation is as effective as the amount of it that gets into the brains of your audience. You may think that it's an opportunity to tell them lots and lots of stuff, but that's wrong. Better to start from making sure your absolute key message hits home and does so effectively; then you can move on to the second most important and so on.

If you are one of those who believe that you have to fill your time allotment full of information, think again; very rarely do you hear anybody come out of a presentation saying that it was too short! In the next chapter, we'll expand on the subject of key messages and look at separating them out from the rest of your presentation content.

Key messages – What?

"What is my message? That is what troubles me. I have not got a message."
William Thomas Stead

In this section we'll look at what on the face of it appears to be a blindingly obvious consideration to any presenter. What are the key messages I wish to impart to the audience? Well would you believe it, some presenters actually craft their stories, rehearse them diligently but haven't actually dissected and analysed what their key messages are.

Key messages are the very core of your presentation. Key messages open the channel that provides direct communication with your audience; these key messages link what your audience already knows with where you are trying to take them. When you stand up to give a presentation, you have a point to make, whether your objective is to educate, discuss, promote or sell. Within every presentation, key messages are the messages you want your audience to remember and react to in the future. Within all your Power Presentation design, key messages keep your 'story' on track with what you are trying to accomplish. Key messages are a means to an end; they assert your viewpoint, confirm facts and educate. Key messages are opinions that you can back up with proof and case examples, which you demonstrate within your presentation.

The key messages within sales and credentials presentations are sometimes known as 'value propositions' – a promise of value to be delivered and a belief from the customer of value that will be experienced. A value proposition can apply to an entire organization, or just parts or departments within it; it can also apply equally to the selling of products or services. According to *Wikipedia*: *Developing a value proposition is based on a review and analysis of the benefits, costs and value that an organization can deliver to its customers, prospective customers, and other constituent groups within and outside the organization. It is also a positioning of value, where Value equals Benefits minus the Cost.*

Whether you are thinking of value propositions or key messages there are, by definition, a maximum of seven absolute cornerstone messages that the entire presentation should be built around. If you are presenting a sales presentation, then the value proposition may well be the key reasons and benefits of buying what you are selling. If you are presenting the results of a market research study, then your key messages could well be the key insights from the project or the actions to take as a result of identifying the insight.

Whatever the topic and format of your presentation, you should begin its design by identifying the key messages you wish to create. We know of any number of excellent Power Presenters who begin the design of their presentations with… the final summary slide of the presentation that contains a final reminder of the key messages only. Then they use each key message as a section heading and build the presentation components around them. Finally they drop in an agenda early on that contains reference to the different sections of the presentation. What this commendable process does is to make sure that the audience are presented with the key messages early in the presentation (when their attention is typically at its highest) and then a number of times throughout to reinforce them and really embed them. They are again given to them once more at the end for good measure. This has proven on many occasions to be an excellent template with which to reliably impart information to an audience.

But before you can build even the framework of your presentation, you need to identify what your key messages are. Clearly this varies by presentation, style and subject matter. It is recommended that you take time looking at all the information you want to impart and then identify what your key points are and remember, no more than seven. Once you accept the Rule of Seven, you'll start to seriously prioritise what is a key message and what is just supporting material. Once you have identified each key message, then give consideration into what is the best order to present them. There are a number of order ideas, but a good option is to find the two most important messages and put one first and the other last, then locate the others in between.

Assuming that you accept the principal of having a set number of key messages before you wade into designing slides and other delivery content, the next thing is to design what your key messages should look like, for maximum impact on the audience. For example, a key message of, *"In the last fiscal year, Acme Corporation like-for-like sales increased from a base of £100,391.35 to £127,361.57"*, would be more impactive if the presenter said those words (missing off the pence though) and at the same time, *"Sales up 27%"* appeared on the screen in a visually impactive way, such as the '27%' aspect being more than 100 in point size.

If the key points can be summarised each into a single short phrase or visual element, then they can be used as the section breaks in the same way. Try to avoid long sentences as these will make the index look like the dreaded list of bullet points. Ideally, you want to try to make the index and summary slides contain an image that the audience can recall that then prompts them as to the key messages from the presentation. For example, you might want to use a five-spoke wheel and each spoke has the prompt to one of your (five in this case) key messages.

In this section, we looked at what and how you should identify the key messages of your presentation and then design the output around them. Typically aim for a maximum of seven messages, use them as the agenda or index, section breaks and as the final summary of your presentation. This way, you'll be ensured of making sure the audience is exposed to your messages as effectively as possible. Incidentally, when first working like this, you might feel that you are putting your key points across too often in your presentation. In our years of Power Presenting, neither we nor any presenters we know have ever reported an audience member making this criticism. But for the most part, they do recall the key messages. So let us take a more detailed look at when to deliver our key messages

Key messages – When?

"If the timing's right and the gods are with you, something special happens."
Rick Springfield

Having now identified the importance of knowing what the key messages of any presentation are and how best to deliver them, let's move on to the subject of when to deliver them. We've already covered the fact that the human brain is best fed information in 20 minute chunks. So where in a particular chunk should the key messages most effectively be located. In the previous section we saw that key messages can be presented near the beginning of a presentation, continually throughout it and then in the final summary. So in answer to the question of when key messages should be delivered, the answer would appear to be a number of times throughout the presentation.

However, there is a particular time in the presentation when the audience's attention is reported to be at its peak. Typically the optimal time to first present your key messages or value proposition is after the initial presenter credibility has been established but not too far into the detail. The rule of thumb is that the audience's attention peaks around five minutes into the presentation. Therefore, as a Power Presenter, endeavour to hit them with your key messages or value proposition at around the five minute marker. By doing this, you'll allow your audience to get accustomed to your presentation style and on-screen content. Also, it gives them time to get comfortable (not too comfortable though) in their seats. Then at around the time they're really tuned in to you and the presentation, POW! Hit them with the key messages or value proposition.

Obviously, this is a rule of thumb and can vary depending on what your key messages are and how they fit into the overall presentation design. But the point we're making here is that you should develop a delivery strategy for your key points in order that they most effectively enter the long term memories of the audience. If you can develop said strategy with an element of psychological science then all the better. The science here is that in a presentation scenario, human attention tends to peak at around five minutes. With that in mind pay particular attention to what you deliver between the four and six minute time markers in your presentation.

So in summary, with regard to when to present the audience with your key messages, the answer is firstly that you should do so at regular intervals throughout your presentation. Secondly, aim to present them for the first time around five minutes from when the presentation commences.

Incidentally, you can also design your presentation to appeal to different emotions of the audience and to take them on a form of emotional roller coaster. For example, when you watch a good film or read a good novel, either entertainment format constantly alters your emotion and it is this in part that holds your attention and makes the story matter more memorable. The same can be said of a good presentation; you want and need your audience to emotionally engage so that they take away more of the content. But for optimal emotional engagement, you need to move people's emotions. Take them from a happy slide to a section with a more sombre tone. Move the audience from a state of relaxation into a more animated state by introducing surprise.

At the times when you know you are actively changing the emotional state of the audience, drop in your key messages or value proposition. This way, you'll retain more interest in your subject matter and at the same time, you will be making sure your key messages are 'pushing on an open door' in terms of presenting them at times when the audience is the most emotionally engaged.

At this stage, we know what our key messages are and when to hit the audience with them. But there's another aspect of presenting that we need to cover and that concerns the attention span of the audience. In the next chapter, we'll quantify how long you have typically got with which to convey your messages to your audience.

Human attention span – 20, 20, 20

"Sixty minutes of thinking of any kind is bound to lead to confusion and unhappiness."
James Thurber

In this section we'll take a look at how long a presentation should be: not in terms of the amount of information that the presenter needs to communicate, but in relation to how much the audience can absorb.

What we're talking about here is human attention span.

As a Power Presenter, you need to structure what you have to present in relation to how much your audience can absorb, and although every person and the style of their presentation can vary, there is a best practice that is wise to adopt. According to a number of (unaccredited) studies the average attention span is around 20 minutes. After that the mind may still retain some information, but a lot of it is lost. In the first 20 minutes, most of the information can be processed more readily and stored into memory by the brain.

There is also a growing bank of evidence that says the best way to present is to break up long data conveyance sessions with soft and hard breaks. A soft break is just an interruption to proceedings that switches attention of the audience away from the subject matter for a couple of minutes. In addition, it's often beneficial to ask the audience to stand up or at least move around. This literally gets the cardiovascular system working and raises blood flow around their bodies. A hard break is more substantial and involves such things as coffee breaks, email and text breaks or opportunities to visit the toilet or take a nicotine hit (for those that still smoke).

So as a rule of thumb, it is wise to either create your presentation so it can be completed in less than 20 minutes or alternatively endeavour to introduce techniques that will have a beneficial impact on the attention of the audience. Our recommendation would be to divide your presentation into 20-minute blocks. That is to say, present content for 20 minutes and then introduce a soft break. Then conduct a second 20-minute block followed by another soft break. After the third 20-minute session, introduce a hard break. Incidentally, we wouldn't advise presenting for more than an hour overall as it is hard for the human brain to remain attentive to the same subject for any longer than this.

As well as dividing your presentation into manageable sessions you can improve audience engagement by taking a number of further steps. Firstly, let your audience know that you are only expecting them to be attentive for 20 minutes. This way, they won't start to mentally wander off just thinking about when this presentation will end. Secondly, recognise and respond to the fact that once you have disengaged the minds of the audience by way of a soft or hard break, it will take a little effort to get them back in the groove again. Once the audience retakes their seats, it's worth just briefly recapping what had been presented before the break and then introducing what will be coming up in the next session. Alternatively, you can always use a stimulating multimedia clip to get the audience attention back onto the core subject matter.

We've already mentioned that attention spans vary by audience and presentation, so another technique you can develop is that of reading your audience. During your presentation try to look out at the audience for clues as to how engaged they are. A room full of heads and eyes fixated on you and the screen indicates that the audience are still with you. Less encouraging signs include lots of looking away from you and your content and people doodling and generally partaking in activities that are just to occupy their minds (as your presentation is no longer doing so). Carrying on from this point, think about how you can tailor the length of your presentation 'on the hoof'. By this we mean incorporate into the design ways to miss out slides and even full sections. One way to do this is to have a 'subtle' navigation bar on screen that lets you hyperlink to various slides or sections. Although effective, this does put content on screen that is of little or no relevance to the audience so isn't ideal. A more professional technique is to have a printed (or better still memorised) list of slide numbers and titles that you can jump to should you need to do so. Then, once you need to move around the presentation because, for example, the audience have become disengaged, simply press the slide number on the keyboard of the hosting computer or laptop and then press enter: Hey presto! The PowerPoint show jumps to that slide.

PowerPoint does offer another navigation tool, but you need to be stood at the lectern and use a mouse to use it ideally. You can right-click your mouse and then on the menu that appears (to you and the entire audience). Then you have the opportunity to 'Go to slide…'

In summary, on the subject of the attention span of your audience, try to keep your blocks of presentation material to 20-minute sessions; and after three of them try to introduce a hard break, such as a chance for refreshments. If you have to present for longer, endeavour to introduce variety onto the screen every 20 minutes or so. This could be in the form of playing multimedia or asking the audience to undertake some type of task. For example, there are now voting systems that work very well and with these, each member of the audience is provided with a keypad and then they get the chance to vote, the results then appear instantaneously on screen. Another example of audience participation is to introduce questions and answers. But be prepared to recognise that if this fails to engage them, then you need to create another break as soon as possible.

Although you can create and deliver a 200-slide deck in one go, for most audiences it will fail to hold their attention past about 20 minutes, so you might as well be presenting to your own bathroom mirror as a worse case example.

Having identified the optimal time for a presentation, so that it can be effectively taken on board by the audience, let's now look at how long you are supposed to present for. Because for some reason or other, the majority of presentation slots aren't in fact 20 minutes in length.

How long is the presentation scheduled for?

"It is my feeling that Time ripens all things; with Time all things are revealed; Time is the father of truth."
Francois Rabelais

The presentation date is set, the venue is set and the time available is set by the conference organiser. What though do you, the presenter, understand by the time available for the presentation? Some key considerations need to be covered to ensure a clear and concise presentation. If the presentation is scheduled to last longer than 20 minutes this in itself has important connotations. The human brain has a maximum attention span of around 20 minutes as we've already discussed, so presentations over this timescale have the danger of key messages getting lost as the audience reaches its collective boredom threshold. If a slot of over 20 minutes is set aside, consider having some form of mental break for the audience, as we discussed in the last chapter. But before that, let's explore the importance of your presentation time slot and how best to use it.

With, say, a 20-minute slot available how many slides does that actually mean as far as the presentation is concerned? We'll look at this a little later on, but here let's just concentrate on how many slides to have. Too many slides and the audience may be visually confused and at worse, won't have time to absorb the information visually thrown at them. Too few slides and the audience may get bored of staring at the one slide and only having to listen. It is important as a presenter to stimulate both the auditory and visual senses of the brain. Getting these two senses working together gives the presenter the opportunity for maximum impact. Whilst there is no fixed rule a good guide as outlined in *Beyond Bullet Points* by Cliff Atkinson is to have one to two slides per minute. This will vary depending on the hierarchical structure applied to the presentation. Incidentally, as a general rule, key message slides should be no longer than sub-level slides.

Having your presentation created and ready to go for a 20-minute presentation may appear as though the job is done, feet can be put up and it's time for a rest. But it would be a mistake to fall into what is a false sense of security. Assuming this presentation has to be used at various venues it is likely that the time available at each venue will vary. From your presentation you need to be clear within that presentation what can be left out and what other slides are available. To become a Power Presenter you must be confident in hiding slides and presenting over various timescales.

The final consideration when presented with a time slot is that of questions and answers. When should these take place and for how long? Allowing ten minutes of questioning during a 20-minute presentation would indicate you were not prepared and did not anticipate the questions when designing the presentation. Too little time for questions and the audience will feel distanced from the presenter. Whilst no fixed rule applies, leave approximately 10-15% of presentation time for questions and answers. If further questions need to be asked make it clear to the audience that you will be available after the presentation to answer questions. Under no circumstances is it acceptable to end your presentation with a question and subsequent answer. By doing this it allows the audience to forget the key message of the presentation. Once the final question is answered make sure you summarise the key messages within the presentation. The audience will then be leaving with those messages reinstated in their memory.

So to summarise, never take the time for a presentation as set. Be prepared to include and drop slides so that the transition for each slide is acceptable to both auditory and visual brain capability. A 20-minute presentation should not be the same as a 15-minute presentation; adaptations need to be included. And finally, be sure the audience leaves the venue with your key message fresh in their memory. This is achieved by not finishing on a question and answer but by using the final minutes to summarise your presentation.

In the last couple of chapters, we've covered a number of aspects of presenting related to time. So let's stay on the subject, but divert our attention to why time is important and how humans (the audience) actually consign information to memory.

Short and long term memory

"The true art of memory is the art of attention."
Samuel Johnson

Before you can craft your prefect Power Presentation, you need to consider how the audience will receive it and, most importantly, what they will remember afterwards. Therefore, let's now explore how we as humans actually remember things. We'll do this by looking at how our memories have developed and why they can be somewhat unreliable. Humans have developed two fundamentally different types of memory: Short term working memory and long term memory. This 'rule of two' is an attempt by evolution to make the brain more fit-for-purpose. As our brains struggle to cope with all that 21st century life has to throw at them, they have to adapt and compromise, often somewhat crudely and inefficiently.

Many thousands of years ago, either up in the trees or balancing on hind legs somewhere in the savannahs of Africa, life was much simpler. Kill or be killed, find a mate and procreate, gather nuts and berries. As a consequence, early man had much less to remember; as time has passed, however, language, numbers and many other abstract concepts, including sitting through presentations, have developed, all actively contributing to human advancement.

Each of these processes, functions and activities takes up some space in the brain and, although something of an over-simplification, all the stuff that people need to remember must be accessible by way of some form of filing system to optimise memory efficiency. To paraphrase Homer Simpson, *"Every time I learn a new stupid thing, something important has to go to make way for it."*

Faced with a life-threatening decision to be made in the blink of an eye, we don't want to root around the archives of our minds for the answers on what course of action to take. Conversely, the words to *Good Ship Lollipop* by Shirley Temple shouldn't be at the forefront of our thoughts every waking hour of our life.

In essence, memory within the human brain can be compared to the different sorts of memory contained in any modern day computer. The basic functions are handled by a human's short term memory, which is similar to how computers use RAM (random access memory), which is very limited in size (comparatively) and is restricted by how much information it can hold at any one time. The long term memory is more like the much larger capacity hard drives that users fill with music, photos, data, and all their learnt and other created things.

In the case of the computer, RAM is supported by what is called 'virtual memory'. This is actually 'borrowed' from the main hard drive to help with software and some hardware functionality. Most of us have at some time or other experienced a computer crash when suddenly the thing locks up and is unable to do anything. Based on my own experience, this typically happens either when scanning the machine for viruses or just moments before a scheduled auto-save was due to occur!

Another analogy to illustrate how our brains function is to think of them as being like a social networking site with each member of the network representing a neuron. When a member sends a message to another member, a connection is made (this is the synapse between different neurons). The more connections a member has, the more connections they can make simultaneously. So, a well-connected member of the social network can communicate to all their connections in a split second.

In essence, this is how the brain does it. What's more, the more often the brain makes the same connection between certain neurons (members), then the more 'hard-wired' (learnt) that connection becomes; in a similar way some social network connections are auto-completed as favourites or friends. What we might see as favourites on social network sites relate to habits when it comes to human brains and these are managed by the brain with little or no conscious awareness or cognitive input.

We can combine the personal computer/human memory analogy with that of the thought process and social networking to explain why we have two memories and how they interlink. We each store all of our social network contact details within our long term memories. In there are all the details about all the people we know. As long as these contacts are online, then the neural pathways are available to make contact with them. When we decide to make contact with an acquaintance in the social network, the short term memory retrieves the minimum amount of detail from the long term memory to enable contact to be made. It then assists in the actual connection, which, once made, it can leave alone.

Although this isn't a perfect analogy, it does summarise the two types of human memory function working together. In the case of the audience's presentation-receiving brains, both short term and long term memories have responsibilities. For example, imagine you are watching and listening to a presenter delivering the usual type of presentation. The long term memory is responsible for processing emotion and the meaning of what is on screen. On the other hand, the short term memory is responsible for processing and comprehending the words spoken and what is on screen.

Crucially, as soon as your short term working memory has finished with its involvement in the process, it erases all the data it used while conducting the screen evaluation and moves on to the next immediate task that you need it to undertake. So as a Power Presenter, you need to make sure that your key messages are not only processed and comprehended by the short term memory, but also embedded into long term memory by making sure they are fully understood and tagged with emotion in some way (covered elsewhere in this book).

In summary, remembering that the red berries are sweet but the green ones are bitter is straightforward and is what our brains are wired to do. Conversely, evaluating what those bar charts mean and how that links to what the presenter is saying, all in the context of having to process the information at a rate not under our own control, starts to scramble our limited brain power.

When it comes to creating and delivering the best Power Presentations, remember that in many occasions the audience will know much less that you, so never assume their level of knowledge. One great feature of the concept of PowerPoint is that if used correctly, it allows even the most complicated of subjects to be explained simply so as to be more memorable for each member of the audience.

Talking of which, in the next chapter we're going to discuss that integral aspect of your presentation, the audience – Specifically, how big is it likely to be?

How many delegates are expected?

"I love an audience. I work better with an audience. I am dead, in fact, without one."
Lucille Ball

When you are creating your presentation have you ever stopped and wondered how many delegates are expected?

The answer to this question will have an impact on the design and presentation style you apply to the overall presentation. For example, does a slide carry the same emphasis on a large projected screen for a large auditorium, as the same slide shown to a small group of delegates on a plasma screen? If care is not taken when designing the presentation, messages can be diluted due to the screen size and distance from the audience.

During this book the use of gesturing to 'welcome' text onto a screen is mentioned. A gesture to a piece of incoming text on a large screen may be lost due to the distance between the presenter and the action on the slide. The distance to a plasma screen or similar display would be acceptable for the gesture to maintain the flow and connection between presenter and presentation.

Consideration also needs to be given to how your overall movement will be channelled or restricted by the number of delegates. For instance, a smaller break-out room may make it extremely difficult to move amongst delegates; if this style of presentation is what was rehearsed then having to change could well disrupt the flow of the presentation.

If a conference organiser is unsure of the exact number of delegates expected when you are designing your presentation then contact the venue directly. Conference centres have to meet fire regulations for maximum occupancy allowed; this can be a starting point with regard to the number of delegates expected. This is particularly important when considering presenting in smaller rooms at hotels or conference centres.

If venues get crowded then a line of sight needs to be established between you, the presenter, and the audience and for the audience to the presentation screen. Having heads bobbing around in the line of sight is only going to create a distraction for the delegates at the back of a room. To solve this possible scenario, arrive at a venue early, assess the room layout and the number of delegates expected for that session and don't be afraid to move the furniture. Establish a layout that as a presenter you feel comfortable with, falling in line with what was rehearsed.

Not only should you endeavour to design your presentation around the likely size of the delegation you are to present to, but you should also factor in whether, and if so how well, they know you, and we'll explore this topic in the next chapter.

Who are my audience? – How well do they know me?

"In communications, familiarity breeds apathy."
William Bernbach

Elsewhere we have talked about the tone and style you adopt so as to be in line with audience expectations. Here we'd like to focus on a specific aspect of how you should alter how you present depending on who you are presenting to.

To begin with, if you are presenting to colleagues who know you well, then they already understand and recognise your personality. They hopefully should also be respectful toward your knowledge of what you are presenting. In this scenario, you needn't worry so much about creating any sort of air of authority or having to deliver your credentials so as to earn their respect (hopefully). In addition, they will be an audience who absorbs your presentation in a way that is congruent with their perception of your own personality.

However, if you are new to your audience, then it is advisable to take a number of steps early in your presentation so as to create the suitable respect and rapport for the messages you are communicating. Here we'll look at three aspects of your presentation that will help you command the optimal air of authority and respect for your presentation. Firstly, we'll cover credentials; secondly the subject of the level of your communication will be discussed; and thirdly, but no less importantly, we'll cover personality.

Firstly, credentials, or in other words how credible you are as a presenter of your content. What we need to do is to establish that we are an authority on our subject matter early on in the presentation so that as the key messages are delivered they are more likely to be accepted at face value, believed and not questioned. For example, if you are selling business-to-business consultancy or expertise, then one way to quickly demonstrate your own credibility is to show a list of your own (well known to the audience) clients; others who you have provided the services to that are known and respected by your audience. You may also wish to add examples of key successes they have achieved as a result of your help and a couple of testimonials (not written on screen, but cited verbally by you). When you have decided how best to present your audience with the reasons why you are credible as a presenter on this subject, don't dwell on the subject as if appearing to boast or gloat. To give an example of this, if you have spoken about your subject matter in a number of different countries, a map of the world and the number on screen is sufficient. The audience don't need for you to list every country, region, college etc. that you have spoken to. Remember that all you are aiming to achieve is their respect at this stage in the presentation.

Often, presenters will put any qualifications they have (relevant to the subject matter) at the back of the presentation as a form of afterthought. We say, if they build your credibility, then get them out there early; even on the cover slide.

The second aspect we want to discuss here is the level of your communication to your audience. What we mean is the way and style in which you deliver your message. For example, you may decide that it's best to talk down to your audience and deliver the message like a king or queen to their subjects. Alternatively, the messages may be better delivered as if chatting to a friend in your local bar. Whatever you decide, there are tricks you can employ to enhance the effect and we'll go through some examples shortly. Firstly, why should the delivery level matter?

To begin with, it may be necessary for you to be a manager of the people you are presenting to or in other words, to be of a higher rank. If you are a new teacher arriving at school, then 'stamping your authority' over a room full of troublesome teenagers may be something you need to do. Conversely, if your presentation relates to some form of team effort, whereby you want the audience to work together and to regard you as part of the team, then you may want to present to them as one of them. One way to do this is to come down from any stage and walk amongst them as you present; looking at the screen from a similar viewpoint to them. You can even sit down with them as you present if you really want to make your point.

If however, you want to appear of higher rank, then start by being physically higher up (such as on a stage) and in this scenario, never sit down with them. Sometimes it may be necessary for you as a presenter to take sides in a presentation. For example, imagine you are representing a certain division of your company and presenting that division's vision for the future, recent performance or whatever. In this situation, consider moving over to wherever other members of that team are in the audience so that you appear to be literally a spokesperson for that team. Also use hand gestures and body language to communication the 'we are a team' message.

The third aspect of this section relates to the personality you present with. Again, if the audience know you quite well, then they will have already a developed perception of your personality, which may or may not be appropriate for your presentation. Just how appropriate your personality is can be measured and worked on if you believe it is an issue, details of which can be found in the Post-Presentation Analysis section of this book.

If however, you and your audience are new to each other, then you need to create a presentation personality. Part of this can be achieved by the style and type of information you use on screen; serious images, dark colours, all very structured in design. Alternatively, using cartoons, lighter, brighter colours and more of a sketchpad, freestyle layout will present a very different personality.

In addition to using your screen style and content to create personality, you can also contribute yourself. Begin by deciding on the tense you use – is it you versus them or all of us together? Are you going to guide and steer them like the Pied Piper? If so, use a tone and language that takes them on a journey with you. Maybe you just need to dish out the orders like a sergeant major. In this scenario, imagine you are just such a being and be as direct and overbearing as you perceive a sergeant major to be.

In summary, taking into consideration the type or types of people in your audience and their knowledge of you at the design stage of your presentation can be a powerful way of creating the most effective way to deliver your key messages. Make sure that they believe you are a credible source of information either by prior experience and knowing you or by getting your credentials in their heads early in your presentation. Secondly, decide on the best level to present. Are you one of them, a leader or boss, or something else? But do make the decision and then try to consistently present in this tone and at this level for much of the presentation (you can, however, soften and be friendlier once all the key messages have been delivered). Finally, understand your presentation personality and develop on what is a congruent and effective means of imparting the type of information you present.

Regardless of the precise details of who you are communicating to, the fact is that mostly they will be other human beings and with that in mind, we're now going to move on to a subject that began some 300 million years ago – Evolution. In the next chapter we'll discover how the way we have evolved still plays a very significant role in dictating what we take notice of and what captures our attention.

Evolution, surprise and what grabs attention

"Evolution is not a force but a process. Not a cause but a law."
John Morley

At its very core, the PowerPoint presentation is a communication tool. As such, it is a tool with which one person communicates with another or others. So let us step back and consider how humans communicate with each other. The heart of the answer to this question lies in the fact that as a species we have evolved over many millions of years and that evolution has shaped how we communicate.

It can also be said that evolution is at the foundation of why we behave as we do, so it's useful to understand exactly what we mean when we talk about evolution. In terms of a dictionary definition, it is the 'change or mutation of inherited traits of a population of organisms (animals or plant life) through successive generations'. When a population splits into smaller groups, these groups evolve independently and develop into new species. Evolution is how man advanced from ape, and it's fascinating to consider how we'll advance to be better equipped to deliver and receive PowerPoint presentations many thousands of years in the future.

From a presentation perspective, *the* key evolutionary development happened relatively recently. Our ancestors first learnt how to talk using a form of human speech in the Upper Palaeolithic period, about 50,000 years ago (we've only been speaking for around 2% of the total time we have been evolving). In other words, speech has only been part of human communication for a fraction of our evolutionary development. As such, our brains aren't naturally wired to think in words, sentences, tonality and the like. We still mentalise things as visual representations. When we see or hear a word or words, our brains need to convert them into something meaningful, a mental image. So, from an evolutionary point of view, your audiences are yet to evolve a natural ability to work with this new-fangled communication contraption known as language (spoken or written). This then supports the famous saying that a picture speaks a thousand words.

Even more recent was the creation of numbers, which were also first used by Palaeolithic peoples around 30,000 BCE. In many ways numbers are much too modern for the brain to have evolved genuine, effective strategies to understand and manage.

Evidence suggests that visual images have been processed by human brains and their evolutionary predecessors for around 10,000 times as long as language and words have been around. Is it any wonder then that so many advertising messages rely on graphic images to get their full message across? But why is it that, in light of this evolutionary limitation, so much PowerPoint communication relies on words to communicate?

As a Power Presenter, you need to help your audiences mentally process the information you are imparting. Remembering that the words you speak (along with your tone of voice and body language) have to be converted into visual mental representations to be understood, the screen should not overload the audience with more words and numbers. Instead, what it needs to do is help the audience make the visual representation of what you are communicating to them. For example, if you want to present the point that something is increasing (such as sales or profits), you can use the screen to visually add the adjective. This way, the audience hears and processes something increasing and they are helped in this processing by the images on the screen offering a pictorial version of increase. In actual fact, it could be argued that graphs and charts are how we have evolutionarily developed to present ranges of data to each other.

The next point to discuss that is directly related to evolution is what most and least effectively gets and holds the attention of human beings. The answer is that for almost all of our evolution, we have been primarily concerned with fight (defend yourself or attack), flight (run away) or find a mate. Our brains are still hard-wired to be ever mindful of these three factors.

As you create your Power Presentations, think about how you can use fight, flight or find a mate to grab the attention of the audience. Advertisers are adept at using sexually suggestive images to draw attention to their messages. They also use fear of threats (fight or flight) in the form of scaring people into thinking that they may be at some sort of risk. You can be as creative as you like creating visual adjectives; a picture of the job centre can instil fear into your employees. Images of children can be used to pull and push all sorts of emotional levers depending on the adjectives you want them to enhance. In actual fact, images of babies are what most women find *the* most visually attractive thing to look at. If you need to get the attention of women, get some babies' faces on the screen! If you are communicating with men, they are more goal and target oriented (and the obvious other parts of adult bodies).

In summary, we human beings are not nearly as sophisticated and developed as we'd like to think we are. And the ways we communicate are deeply rooted in our own evolution over millions of years. For that reason, we respond and react most to images and messages that are related to fighting, fleeing or finding a mate: All combine to ensure the survival of us as a species. Power Presenters are those who can communicate their messages the most effectively and using evolutionary hard-wiring is a great way of doing this. Secondly, remember that humans have yet to fully evolve to naturally use words, language and numbers. Graphs can simplify how you present numeric information so that the audiences can more easily mentally process it. Images used as visual adjectives can be beneficial if you need to get what you are saying to be embedded in the brains of those in the audience. As one final point, this section has once again provided evidence that bullet points shouldn't be visible on a PowerPoint screen during a presentation.

Although emotional responses are still based on fight, flight or find a mate, it is possible for you to manage how the audience emotionally responds to you and your presentation. In the next chapter, we'll explain what an emotion is and armed with that understanding, how you can dramatically improve the emotional engagement and rapport between you and your audience.

Emotions and connecting with the audience

"Possession of the 'truth' is less important than emotional sincerity."
George Orwell

It is impossible to escape the fact that as human beings, we are emotional. In fact, almost every decision that we make, we do so emotionally and not rationally. So as you sit in an audience absorbing a presentation, you are constantly filtering the contents, including how it is delivered, through your own emotions. At a fundamental level, unless you have an emotional connection to what you are seeing and hearing, there is little chance of it getting past your short term memory and embedding itself into your long term memory. Understanding and working with the emotions of the audience are absolutely pivotal to all Power Presenters.

Let's begin by defining what we mean when we talk about emotions. They are the building blocks of feelings and are with all of us, all of the time, to a greater or lesser extent. As our minds develop, we each create our own personalised inner world based on our experiences.

In more technical terms, an emotion is the complex combined psychological and physiological response of a person to a single stimulus or set of incoming stimuli. It is the response of the brain and body to create a state of readiness to respond to a particular stimulus or set of stimuli (fight or flight for example). In humans, emotion fundamentally involves physiological arousal, expressive behaviours and conscious experience. According to Robert Plutchik, author of *Emotions and Life*, and Professor Emeritus at the Albert Einstein College of Medicine and Adjunct Professor at the University of South Florida, emotions are genetically based, unlearned behavioural adaptations that have value for the individual; they are patterned reactions rather than disorganised events.

Before there can be any form of physiological response to an incoming stimulus or set of stimuli, there has to be a form of psychological evaluation. In other words, before the hairs on the back of our neck can stand on end, our brain has to send the appropriate impulses for that physiological 'behaviour' to occur. For our brain to send out such a signal it first has to receive the stimuli that it needs to respond to; these stimuli are received from one or more of the five senses. Each of the senses is physiological by nature, so in essence the process of an emotional reaction goes like this: 1, incoming physiological stimulus; 2, almost instantaneous psychological processing; 3, if appropriate, a signal goes back to the physiological system(s) to do something. Body first, then brain, then back to body.

How do our brains process and decode the incoming physiological stimuli? They do so by using a somewhat basic evolutionarily-based calculation: Chase it to eat, chase it to mate, or will it chase me and eat me? Based on the outcome of the calculation, the brain can decide which part of the body needs the blood, oxygen and nutrients to best address the situation. In other words, our brains take even the most complex physiological stimuli, such as watching an expensively crafted PowerPoint presentation with all of its multimedia capabilities and then take it all the way back to fight, flight or fornicate.

Emotions are built on three different psychological components, which all appear to a greater or lesser extent in all emotions. First, there is enjoyment, happiness or pleasure; there will be lots of enjoyment in glee, but hardly any in anger for example. The second aspect or component of an emotion is excitement, stimulation or arousal. Emotions of confrontation contain a high percentage of excitement, whereas being obliging would contain a minimal amount. The third and final psychological component that exists in every emotion is intimidation, or conversely, control or dominance; how in control of a situation a person feels. Greed and impulsivity are both emotions that contain high levels of control while obedience and shyness would only contain high levels of intimidation.

These three components of emotion, enjoyment, excitement and intimidation, are the mental switches that the brain uses to prepare the body for an instinctive course of action. As an analogy, imagine that these three components of emotion are the ingredients needed to make a traditional homemade wine: grapes, sugar and yeast. Depending on how much of each ingredient is used in proportion to the other two, determines what the final wine will be like. Too much of one ingredient and the wine may turn out bitter. Get the balance wrong another way and the mixture may explode out of the barrel. However, get the balance of ingredients just right and the result is a balanced, tasty and enjoyable wine.

As we absorb a presentation (or in fact deliver one) we are constantly receiving stimuli through our nervous systems that are in turn being instantly processed by the fight, flight or fornicate parts of our brains. On the one hand, it is important that the stimuli are correctly converted into an appropriate emotional response and on the other hand, it is possible that by manipulating the stimuli we receive, our emotional responses can be influenced and altered.

To recap, an emotion is the combined complex psychological and physiological experience that results from a person reacting to a particular single stimulus or set of stimuli they encounter. Emotions are the split-second changes in mental and physical states that come directly from the evolutionary development of man.

With this new-found expertise regarding emotion, the next time you begin to design a presentation start to consider those key aspects of audience response: Enjoyment, excitement and intimidation (EEI). You can now begin to design more appropriate emotions to align with your key messages. For example, good news should be enjoyable, with a sprinkling of excitement and not much intimidation. What does this mean in terms of a presentation design? Firstly, any imagery that portrays enjoyment should be in colour, brightly lit, larger than life and communicate happiness (such as smiling faces of people). Excitement can be generated by adding images of excited faces to the screen content or simply delivering the message while adopting an excited manner yourself. Intimidation can be avoided by not using too many capital letters and by avoiding appearing to talk down to the audience.

We're not advocating that you become experts on emotion in order to be a Power Presenter; more that by consciously thinking of how your presentation, including content and delivery, will make the audience feel (emotionally) and thus will lead to much more emotionally engaging results. Ergo, more of your key messages will successfully find their way into the long term memories of the audience. In fact, it's pretty much the only way they'll get there.

Next, we'll look at what it is that motivates each and every one of us (over and above fundamental emotional stimuli). When we combine our emotional needs with our 'intelligent' cognitive ability, we arrive at a set of drivers, at least one of which will be at the very heart of how we arrive at decisions – consequences that impact on each of us at a personal level.

Meet audience needs – Central six fitness indicators

"Humans may never give up their drives for status, respect, prestige, sexual attractiveness and social popularity."
Geoffrey Miller

From an evolutionary perspective, there are six key drivers that all humans are motivated by. Naturally, if you can tailor your presentation to cover each of these evolutionary drivers, then it's highly likely that you will more effectively engage your audience.

These drivers are based on how we want the rest of the world to perceive us and what we think is most important. They are very powerful levers that we each have in our minds and that significantly influence our likes, dislikes and beliefs. But before introducing the 'central six', or the six universal fitness indicators, consider the following: Human beings are remarkably similar to each other. Each has a similar number of chromosomes (23), just over 600 muscles, more than 200 bones and, according to Geoffrey Miller, can expect to take 600 million breaths over the average lifespan. But, as American psychologist William James points out: *"There is very little difference between one man and another, but what there is, is very important."*

Over the last 100 years, numerous psychologists have identified that there are just six different aspects of human behaviour, which are the key differences that distinguish human minds from each other.

Geoffrey Miller, in his book *Must-Have*, refers to the six fitness indicators as follows: general intelligence, openness to experience, conscientiousness, extraversion, agreeableness and emotional stability.

These core fitness indicators are an excellent means of linking the evolutionary needs of humankind (survival, mating and sociability) with modern day presentation subjects. Looking at the central six in more detail, the first is general intelligence, which appears to be a relatively good guide or index to genetic quality. According to Miller, general intelligence correlates positively with overall brain size, speed of performing motor tasks, physical health, mental health, sperm quality and therefore romantic attractiveness. If your audience is able to relate aspects of your presentation content to their own general intelligence (and boost it if possible), then they will perceive the content worthwhile and more personally beneficial.

The second of the central six fitness indicators is extraversion, which indicates the degree to which a person is outgoing, friendly, talkative and socially confident. Extraverts tend to enjoy leading, prefer to be active and exhibit higher levels of self-confidence. People who are low in extraversion prefer to work alone, tend to be physically passive and are less trusting; low extraversion is associated with negativity and shyness. From a presentation point of view, you should allow your audience to view your presentation equally as a leader or a follower; in other words, neither dictate nor fawn as you present. Adopt a neutral middle ground and let the audience find their own preferred level of receiving the information.

Openness is the third of Geoffrey Miller's fitness indicators and relates to the curiosity, novelty seeking and broadmindedness of people. Depending on our openness, we'll tend to perceive others who we see as less open as dull, tedious or boring. Conversely, we'll probably regard those who appear more open than us as threats; bizarre, eccentric and even downright mad. Although many of us have a tendency to try to appear more open than we are, the truth is that most of us have a natural comfort level of openness and we seek others of a similar nature. This takes a degree of managing when it comes to Power Presenting and links back to what is on the slide and how you convey your aspect of the presentation. In essence, try not to be all whizz bang with random animations all over the place. Equally, don't make the slides and your delivery too boring. As a rule of thumb, endeavour to cover these three design guidelines: 1, something on the screen that is unexpected (or the way you present it); 2, an overall message with a co-ordinated build and in a consistent style; and 3, the one single thing you want the audience to take away from that slide.

The fourth of Geoffrey Miller's six fitness indicators is conscientiousness. This is the personality trait that includes such characteristics as punctuality, reliability, integrity and trustworthiness. Conscientiousness is essentially the self-control exerted by the frontal lobes in the brain onto the much more impulsive, short term and selfish instincts of the limbic system. According to Miller, conscientiousness is slow to mature, but when it does, it inhibits the short term mating activity that tends to maximise reproductive success among younger human males. Because conscientiousness is managed by the more recently-evolved frontal lobes of the brain, it is argued that this trait wasn't needed or even prevalent in the prehistoric hunter–gatherer life. In terms of presenting, this fitness indicator is all about accuracy and consistency: Accurate data, consistent fonts and every aspect of the slide in the pixel perfect correct location (no jumping graphics as you move from slide to slide just because you were 10 pixels out when you pasted an image onto a slide).

Geoffrey Miller refers to the fifth fitness indicator as agreeableness. He states that agreeableness is at the very heart of human altruism and social progressivism. In other words, it is the rare product of natural selection and sexual selection that allows us to rise above the instincts of most of the animal kingdom. Highly agreeable people want to get along with as many people as possible, so they tend to conform. When designing and delivering your Power Presentation don't be too radical. Although you want some design on view, don't overdo it – try to make sure things like colours actually match or contrast correctly.

The sixth and final fitness indicator is that of emotional stability. This refers to the resilience we have, how resistant we are to stress and how quickly we can mentally recover from an emotional setback. Those of us who are emotionally stable tend to be calm, relaxed, optimistic and quick to come to terms mentally with a given situation. Those with low emotional stability are more likely to exhibit anxiousness, depression and pessimism. They are quick to anger, tend to cry with little or no encouragement and suffer from anxiety. In this aspect, you need to be aware of how your Power Presentation will impact the audience emotionally and whether this is congruent with the key messages you are delivering. For example, you don't want to present bad news in a comedic way, neither do you want to make light of significant achievements your company has made.

If and when an audience member is of the belief that accepting and taking on board the messages you are conveying is worthwhile, then they will be able to use the output to enhance other people's perception of their own personal general intelligence, openness to experience, conscientiousness, extraversion, agreeableness or emotional stability; then your presentation is much more likely to 'hit the spot'.

So far we've talked a lot about you communicating your messages to your audience and how to get them to most effectively take them on board. Now let's get under the hood and start to talk about the presentation itself. And where better to start than Slide 1? In the next chapter, we'll detail a number of important aspects of this apparently innocuous part of the presentation that we urge you to take on board.

The front cover slide: It has a number of objectives – Don't skimp

"For, usually and fitly, the presence of an introduction is held to imply that there is something of consequence and importance to be introduced."
Arthur Machen

When you create a new presentation, how much thought do you give to the cover slide or front cover? If you are like the majority of PowerPoint users, probably not a lot. Typically, front covers contain a presentation title, maybe the presenter's name and company name plus some auto text such as the date.

In this section, we'll explore the full potential of the cover slide and offer advice as to how you and your audience can get more out of it and benefit from its existence. So let's look at how you can use the slide for your own benefit as a presenter and at the same time, some of the benefits it offers your audience. Typically, this is the slide that will be in front of your audience for a period of time before the presentation commences. Also, it is a slide where some text is not just permitted, but advised, so don't miss out. You can offer your audience a name for the presentation and a description of what to expect (only a single, short sentence though). This helps manage their expectations and assists with any nerves about forgetting your opening lines that you may experience.

The cover slide can also help in portraying your personality, style and perhaps some panache if designed professionally. The audience will begin to develop their perceptions of what sort of presentation they are in for and even what they think of the presenter, just by looking at the cover slide of the presentation. So from your point of view as a presenter, design the cover slide to represent the tone of the presentation and how you want the audience to anticipate what the content will be and the style in which it will be delivered.

In terms of a few dos and don'ts, firstly, avoid clip art as there are many, many more professional looking and more effective images on the Internet (*Google Images* for example). Secondly, if you have always used auto text, then just ask yourself why? Is there any benefit of the audience knowing the precise file location of the presentation? Probably not. If, like a lot of PowerPoint users, you haven't been classically trained in design, then simply imitate the works of those who have. Look at covers for films on DVDs, books and the introductions to television programmes. Try to copy the layouts, colour schemes, fonts and any illustration style. Chances are that by taking this approach, your covers will improve significantly. Another best practice tip is not to feel compelled to fill all the empty areas on the cover slide (or any slide for that matter) with logos and the like. Your slides should have plenty of 'white space' and the cover especially so.

Another don't relates to PowerPoint templates: Don't use them. Most templates included in PowerPoint will have been seen by your audience countless times. What's more, a lot of the templates are not all that great to begin with. Your audience expects from you a unique presentation with new (at least to them) content.

There is another way in which the cover slide can help both your credibility and confidence before you even stand up. It can communicate your job title (providing it is suitably professional that is) and/or any relevant membership(s) you may possess. If, like countless other PowerPoint users, you aren't blessed with an auspicious job title, then be creative: *Key account manager* sounds better than *sales person*, for example. *Leading authority* comes across more professionally than *company representative*.

In summary, spend time and give serious consideration to what it is you want your cover slides to communicate. Think about how they can help you as a presenter and how they can manage expectations and pre-presentation perceptions of the audience.

Continuing in the vein of communication, we're now going to discuss the pace at which you communicate: Not simply how fast you talk on stage, but more scientifically, the rate at which your audience can absorb and adequately retain new information. In the next chapter, cognitive load thresholds will be explored and how, as a consequence of understanding human limitations, you can optimise the pace with which you impart information to your audience.

Providing too much information too quickly

"A brain is a lot like a computer. It will only take so many facts, and then it will go on overload and blow up."
Erma Bombeck

Presenters can and do get all excited and wrapped up about presenting loads of information; it makes them look good, feel clever etc. However, in this section, we'll explore the fact that humans have a limitation with regard to the pace at which they can take information on board. As a result, we as Power Presenters need a template for making sure we pace the feed of information at an acceptable level, and that depends on the type of audience.

A simple way to manage the pace at which you deliver information to your audience is to simply use your voice for the detail and the screen to just make or enhance the headline point. In these next chapters however, we'll offer a more step-by-step approach to managing data flow.

Let's start by explaining the science: In their book, *Efficiency in Learning*, Ruth Clark, Frank Nguyen and John Sweller define the speed and amount of information a person can process and then learn (known as Cognitive Load Theory) as a 'universal set of learning principles resulting in an efficient instructional environment as a consequence of leveraging human cognitive learning processes'. Or to put it so you can cognitively understand the last sentence – Cognitive Load Theory explains how to make complex things easy to understand. It is based on understanding how those trying to learn actually process incoming information to retain it for future use (remember it). The incoming new information is broken down into manageable sized 'packets' that can be processed and embedded into the brain. In other words, we aren't able to learn a new dance routine instantly, but we can learn two or three dance steps at a time. The number of steps we can learn depends on a number of factors including intelligence, interest in the subject matter and learning environment (in a dance studio or on a bus). The learning ability of a particular person or group of people to a particular subject is known as their 'cognitive load threshold'.

Cognitive load thresholds vary by individual and by familiarity with the subject matter; a good example of how the cognitive load threshold changes can be illustrated by thinking back to when we first learnt to drive a car. When you're first behind the wheel the process is very alien. For a beginner, driving a car is a mentally draining series of conscious evaluations and adjustments. As a new driver we constantly have to evaluate any number of situations and soon become cognitively 'full'. However as time passes, driving appears to become easier and even second nature. This is because groups of behaviours have been chunked together, which reduces the input needed from the short term working memory. What we find so mentally taxing and stressful as a new driver can be handled with ease once we've been driving for a while. As more experienced motorists, we can not only drive with much less mental effort, but can also hold a conversation, listen to the radio, take a drink from a bottle of water and more. Some people are so comfortable that they even think they could shave, put on make-up or even change their clothes, which is needless to say, highly illegal and dangerous!

So bringing this into the realm of Power Presenting, we need to recognise and estimate the cognitive load threshold of our audience and then feed the information to them at an acceptable level. For example, a room full of clinical psychologists will be able to absorb more information about all things psychology related than the typical audience at one of those inspirational pseudo-psychologically related 'think and grow rich' events.

There is one particular tool that not enough presenters use sufficiently well, and that is silence. Make your point and then give the audience time to process, analyse and digest it. The design of the slide can be a great benefit to you if your aim is to present a manageable cognitive load to the audience. This is where the slide build can really help. Instead of hitting the audience with a broadside of stuff to mentally process, feed it in bit by bit so that it builds into a clear and easily memorable visual story, narrated by you the presenter. For example, you put a single statistic on the screen (72%) and tell the story that it refers to (the fact that sales are up by that amount in the last quarter); in return the audience will find it easier to manage the input of information and so confine it to long term memory, remembering an image of 72% and then the audio that went with it.

Another effective technique to manage the speed at which you impart information is to look at all the data you want to convey and then work on reducing it down by as much as possible visually. For example, let's explore the basics of charts. Most presenters are guilty of simply having too much data in their on-screen charts and although there are lots and lots of different chart types, once again there are a few best practice rules we can follow. Use pie charts to show percentages and limit the number of slices to no more than six. In addition, you can add emphasis to your point by exploding the key percentage slice out of the chart or just colouring it in a contrasting tone to the remainder of the slices.

Vertical bar charts are good for presenting changes over time (such as sales or quantities). Horizontal bar charts are better used to compare quantities (such as sales between offices or regions). Line charts are an effective way of presenting trends and can be further enhanced by incorporating arrows along the trend line.

Tables aren't naturally effective in presentations and for that reason should really be used only if you want to minimise the impact of the data you are presenting. In our experience, tables are best left in reports or handouts and shouldn't be used on screen.

In summary, your audience can only mentally absorb so much information and the job of the Power Presenter is to understand the likely cognitive load threshold of the audience and deliver their key messages within it. This can be achieved both in the amount of information imparted, the speed at which it is delivered and the way in which the presenter and their screen work in tandem.

Now let's turn the tables and in the next chapter, we'll provide details of how you can actually confuse your audience, but to positive effect. We'll show you how you can increase mental focus and engagement towards your presentation pretty much any time you like. Once again, tried and tested psychology provides the foundation for this next presentation technique.

Cognitive dissonance

"The eye sees only what the mind is prepared to comprehend."
Robertson Davies

There is a very powerful but somewhat underused presentation technique that we'd like to discuss here. The tool is based on a psychological term known as 'cognitive dissonance', which is defined as a 'discomfort caused by holding conflicting cognitions (e.g. ideas, beliefs, values, emotional reactions) simultaneously'. One of the best examples of this can be seen in an early study and has been described by Leon Festinger *et al* in the book *When Prophecy Fails*. In this example, a religious group was expecting the imminent end of the world on a certain date. When that date passed without the world ending, the movement did not disband. Instead, the group came to believe that they had been spared in order to spread their teachings to others, a justification that resolved the conflict between their previous expectations and reality.

So how does cognitive dissonance work in the realms of presentation creation and delivery? Basically it's all about creating a managed form of audience confusion so that their attention is held and even increased. The aim here is to present an audience with information that on the surface doesn't make any sense; said information can be spoken but is often better presented visually, on screen. For example, if the screen shows a message such as "The 5 golden rules" and at the same time, there are just the numbers 1 to 4 or four speech bubbles, circles, graphics or whatever on screen, then the audience is forced to do more mental processing to make sense of what's in front of them. Ergo, their attention is retained. As the presenter then develops the five golden rules story, the audience pays attention as they wait for either the presenter to foul up and admit there are only four, or more often, revealing a fifth golden rule verbally (and justifying why it wasn't in the on-screen list).

To a lot of presenters, the very thought of presenting an incomplete sentence or diagram sends shudders down their pedantic spines. But in the arena of Power Presenting, an incomplete sentence does definitely not amount to an incomplete presentation. Not, that is, if your intention is to get the audience thinking, more mentally engaged and attentive. And as many scientists and presentation professionals will attest, when we as a species have to give serious attention and thought to something, then the results are that we remember more about it and we actually remember the details longer. When you are designing slides this is an amazingly powerful technique to include as it has been proven on numerous occasions to optimise audience attention.

Another form of cognitive dissonance would be to say to the audience, "Look at the four squares on the screen", and as they do, only three appear. While they spend time mentally processing the dissonance, you explain the meaning of the three squares and then, hey presto, introduce a fourth (perhaps a big square encompassing the other three). Bingo! The slide now makes sense to the audience and you've had their full attention as you delivered it.

And this is a key aspect to using cognitive dissonance – it must come together in a way that makes sense at the end. Otherwise, you've achieved little more than audience confusion. When this does happen, the audience will still be mentally trying to solve the past slide after you've moved on and so their attention will have waned.

Another point to make with regard to cognitive dissonance is that some presenters lack sufficient confidence to brazenly present what appear to be inaccuracies on screen and will immediately explain what they are about to reveal. This then removes the need for the audience having to remain attentive and so takes away the effectiveness of the tool. If and when you introduce cognitive dissonance, do so with confidence. The key is to increase and retain audience attention, so as long as you make it all clear and come together at the end of the slide it is a very effective tool.

Like so many things related to presenting in public, this tool can be used to both good and bad effect. In other words, cognitive dissonance can be negative as well as positive. A classic example being when any data on screen is factually incorrect. Although this is permissible if the presenter meant it to be and has a clever patter to explain the error. But when the data is just plain wrong, then the audience disengages from the key messages of the presentation, as they try to make sense of the error and if they don't, they lose faith in the presentation to a greater or lesser extent.

Another form of negative cognitive dissonance is when a presenter goes off on a subject as a new slide is presented to the audience only to realise after some seconds (or minutes) that the slide isn't what they had expected and so the spoken word and the on-screen content don't match. If this happens to you and you have created inadvertent cognitive dissonance, be careful how you extricate yourself from this pickle. If you want to deliver an excuse as to why you got it wrong, then make it plausible if possible. But don't be afraid to front up to the fact that you've cocked up, as there is a famous proverb that says something like: *"He who has never made a mistake has never tried or achieved anything."* Conversely, if at the moment you find yourself at home to *Mr. Foul Up* and you decide to lie your way out of it, then lie with conviction, and no half measures.

The key points relating to cognitive dissonance are firstly that it is a great tool to manage the attention of the audience, which can lead to significantly higher recall of presentation content later on. When you develop the skills to use it well, your presentations will improve significantly. But as with all things presentation related, be careful not to introduce negative cognitive dissonance such as factually incorrect information on screen.

While looking into the workings of the human brain, the next chapter continues this theme and explores just how limited our apparently advanced mental processing ability actually is. Recognise how much the brains of your audience can manage and then be able to design your presentation accordingly.

Human brain limitations

"If the brain were so simple we could understand it, we would be so simple we couldn't."
Watson Lyall

In this next chapter, we'll explain and quantify the very limited processing power of the human brain (particularly the short term memory related part). In addition, we'll provide the science behind it in terms of what 7±2 mental processing means in relation to presenting PowerPoint and how it necessitates slide building and the strict pacing of information imparting.

So to begin with, the fact is that the human brain is severely restricted with regard to the amount of information it can process at any one time. The amount of information we could simultaneously process was believed to be seven, plus or minus two. A piece of information could be any stimulus that needs some degree of conscious processing and that reaches our awareness from any of the five senses (visual, auditory, kinaesthetic, olfactory or gustatory).

This magic number (7±2) was first identified by the cognitive psychologist George A. Miller of Princeton University's Department of Psychology. He argued that the number of objects an average human can hold in short term working memory is 7±2. As civilisation has evolved, our brains find it increasingly difficult to cope more efficiently with all the tasks expected of them. In essence, our short term working memory struggles to handle all the aspects of the 21st century.

A second limitation of the human brain relates to memory span. This refers to the longest list of items (e.g. digits, letters, words) that a person can repeat back immediately after presentation. George A Miller (again) quantified that the memory span of young adults is approximately 7 items. He noticed that memory span is approximately the same for stimuli with vastly different amounts of data. For example, binary digits have 1 bit each; decimal digits have 3.32 bits each; words have about 10 bits each. Miller concluded that memory span is not limited in terms of bits but rather in terms of chunks. A chunk is the largest meaningful unit in the presented material that the person recognizes – thus, it depends on the knowledge of the person as to what counts as a chunk.

Now we can see a direct correlation between generally perceived best practices for presentations with the solid science behind it.

Many agree that there should be only a few words either on screen or in the dreaded bullet point (typically six). It's no coincidence that this number six equates so well to how much we as a species can mentally process. You can take this figure and work with it in your future presentation designs and deliveries.

Be mindful of never expecting the audience to process more than six bits of information at any one time. Remember also, that information is not just visual; it can be sounds, feelings, smells and tastes too. In fact you can use the multi-sensory processing to your benefit because separate research has identified that people can process multi-sensory input more efficiently.

A good guide is to look at each slide you have designed and to quantify how much information you are expecting the audience to take on board at any one time. If the number is above seven, then seriously consider splitting the content into two or more slides.

As we've seen, we can manage the human frailty of having limited mental processing power by feeding the information across to the audience at a manageable rate. A means by which we can achieve this is to let each bit or byte of information on a slide build to deliver an overall message at the end. In the next chapter, we'll explore ways of using the contents of a slide to build towards a complete story or message.

Building slides

"Storytelling is the most powerful way to put ideas into the world today."
Robert McAfee Brown

In this next chapter, we're going to explore the matter of building slides; this relates to being able to build a slide to tell a story as opposed to just going 'splat' there it all is. By definition, what we mean by building a slide is when a slide first appears on screen, there is nothing or only a single 'message' on it (perhaps just the title). Then the presenter talks through the slide, and as they do so, they click and add more content, so much at a time, and so visually emphasising the narrative story they are telling.

The headline objective of a slide that builds in front of an audience as the presenter tells the tale is to help the audience to remember to do something. You hit an audience with too much information too fast and they'll close down, and as a result remember next to nothing. Alternatively, if you craft and build the slide point by point (not bullet point by bullet point though), then the audience can process the information you are communicating at a much more acceptable speed and so embed more into their memories.

We often get asked how it is possible to remove most of the text from a slide and still make it impactive and memorable. Firstly, let's go back to basics; presenting slides with paragraphs of text is just about the worst thing you can do to an audience. If anybody really wanted to read your text, then they'd have been better to receive an email or report, or 'buy the book'. The fact is that no audience member wants to read your text. Furthermore, and as we've explained elsewhere in this book, for most people it is an impossibility to even pay attention to a large amount of text on a slide, let alone process what is being communicated, and simultaneously concentrate on what the presenter is saying. They simply can't do it: Pretending otherwise is both an affront to the time and effort they have invested in turning up and an insult to them.

So back to the question of how to reduce text and yet present information effectively. Get rid of as much of your current text as possible and find methods of displaying the same ideas in visual ways. Why not use pictures, graphs, video clips, and so forth. PowerPoint has been created to present visually and graphically, therefore, don't be afraid to harness its true potential. By doing so, you more effectively feed into the audience's brain's mechanisms for processing non-verbal information.

When building a slide, try to limit the content to a single main idea per slide and then develop it. Here is a fact that some may not realise – PowerPoint presentations don't physically burst at the seams if there are too many slides in a deck. So why presenters feel the urge to cram so much information onto the same slide is baffling. Much better to add another slide than overcrowd the initial one. I'll bet you've all heard a presenter say something like: "I'm not sure if you can all read the numbers in this chart..." If the presenter already doubts the legibility of his or her own material, then why on earth go ahead and present it?

Start by presenting a single point and then develop means and ways of emphasising and contextualising it visually, using the screen build. By reducing the on-screen content to a single idea or message per slide, you'll significantly improve both your own performance as a presenter and the *memorability* of what you present.

Another reason why too many presenters feel obliged to put too much information onto each slide is because there is an invisible timer somewhere that makes presenters think that each slide takes a certain amount of time to get through, multiply that up by the number of slides and the result is how long it will take to finish the presentation. I recently attended a 30-minute presentation on what was a complex topic related to estate agency or realty. During the presentation, the entire audience remained fully engaged with the subject and in the coffee break afterwards seemed to have taken on board all that was presented. So how many slides did the presenter use? One! It built slowly and deliberately to unfold a clear and engaging set of messages in the form of a good story. So the message here is that it is hard to have too few slides in a presentation, if you let them each build in a way that keeps the audience engaged.

In another example, we observed a presenter use more than 30 slides in just 10 minutes on stage, and guess what? Their presentation was equally effective. So in summary here, what we're saying is that there are no rights and wrongs in terms of numbers of slides. Rather, that each slide should be treated as a scene in a film or chapter in a book, unfolding and developing right before the eyes of the audience.

It could be argued that the PowerPoint workspace is misleading as it gives designers slides to fill in the first place. Other applications such as Flash use frames, and then they get played back at so many frames per second, like a video clip. Don't let the PowerPoint slide dominate the timescale; after all, they can be as brief as single frames in a movie if the presenter can advance them quickly enough.

As a final point relating to building slides, those of you who are familiar with PowerPoint will no doubt know about the 'Select Pane' on the ribbon at the top of the screen (on the home screen). For those of you who may not be aware, this is a great way to design slides from the back to the front as it allows designers to hide items on screen one at a time. For example, if you have a chart at the back of your screen and then cover it up with various other visual elements, for many it appears hard to get to later on if you want to make changes. Using the Select Pane allows you to hide everything you want, item by item until all that is on screen is what you want to edit.

As a summary of building slides, pace the rate of information you put on screen, don't overcrowd the screen and be willing to add more and more slides. Try to keep it to a single message per slide and then use the build to develop the message so that it becomes embedded in the brains of the audience.

Continuing on from discussing things appearing on screen, let's turn our attention to how those items appear. In the next chapter, we'll take a look at animation and explore aspects of the good, the bad and the downright ugly.

Animation dos and don'ts

"Animation can explain whatever the mind of man can conceive. This facility makes it the most versatile and explicit means of communication yet devised for quick mass appreciation."

Walt Disney

In this next chapter, we'll focus on another well established *PowerPointism* – Animation. Should text, graphics, clips or images fade in, fly in, spin in, or whatever? There is a wealth of options available, but before clicking on the insert animation button, let's introduce some ground rules. Firstly, only use animation of any form if it helps to make a point or emphasizes the key messages you are delivering. Don't use animation just to make your presentation more interesting; that is the job of the content and the way you as a presenter deliver it. Secondly, don't use too many different animation effects. Although the audience likes to see a professional slideshow develop in front of them, they do prefer to have some order to it.

There are a couple of tools you can use with regard to animation best practice. If you have text entering the screen (not too much though) try to feed it in, in a logical manner. In the western world, we read from left to right, so with regard to text, feed it in from the left of the screen and, if possible, have your body located to the side so as to create the effect of the text leaving your body and entering the screen. The other tool to consider here is movement. In PowerPoint, objects on screen can fade in/out, grow and shrink, spin and a host of other options are available. But as humans are still mentally hard-wired for fight, flight or find a mate ('the 3Fs'), our brains are constantly monitoring our surroundings for movement. If we sense any, we'll focus in on it and process it from a 3F perspective. So what this means in relation to Power Presenting is that any movement on screen will attract attention and this can be both good and bad. If you want to draw attention or emphasize a particular part of the screen, then adding animation can be a good thing. Conversely, if you want to reduce the impact and visibility of some aspect on screen, then have other parts of the screen animated to divert the audience's attention away from what you don't want them to focus on. For example, in the financial services industry there are so many mostly negative messages that have to be shown to customers and potential customers, that they can make any related sales presentation very negative. But if the viewer is encouraged to focus away from these points, then there is more chance of them remaining positive and so being more susceptible to buying something.

There is another set of animations that occur as slides change from one to another. In PowerPoint, these are known as transitions. You should mainly use these to create impact at the moment when one slide replaces another. However, as usual, there are a couple of considerations. Firstly, once you decide on a transition to use in a presentation, try to only use that one and use it between each and every slide change. In summary, if you use slide transitions, then use just one (or two at the most).

When it comes to choosing which transition(s) to adopt, avoid the flashier ones, as too much movement will distract your audience. PowerPoint has a transition feature that the majority of experts agree is not beneficial to presentations and that is the 'Random' transition effect. With this you have no idea which effect will come next, but one thing is pretty much certain, it'll be different to the last one (how annoying and distracting is that?).

Back to the subject of animations, the final key consideration is about timing and control. Here you want to be in full control of what happens and when. Try not to be forced to rely on the computer processor speed as to when an animation will occur. Much better to control it with a presentation clicker discreetly in your hand; then you can click at the precise moment you want something to happen and, hey presto, it will. In the animations settings arena, you can choose whether you want the animation to occur automatically or on the click of a mouse (or presentation clicker). We advise that you go for the latter wherever possible so that you retain control of what's going on.

PowerPoint has a plethora of options with regard to timings, animation and otherwise. As a rule of thumb, we suggest you ignore pretty much all of them. Once you start having the slide itself dictate your delivery then you've lost control. Even the smallest thing such as someone in the audience sneezing or their mobile phone ringing can throw off the timings and they can be almost impossible to get back in sync. In summary, however much you are encouraged or feel the urge to automate timings, resist the temptation because generally speaking the result is a higher probability of the presentation going wrong somehow.

On the subject of animation and transition timings, you can set predetermined speeds for them to occur (slow, medium and fast). Typically, these animations and changes should be short and sweet. If you present your audience with an animation that takes 10 seconds or so to complete, then chances are they'll become frustrated and start to disengage.

As a final point regarding animations and transitions, when considering them, keep your audience in mind. In a glitzy presentation for sales and marketing sorts, you can probably indulge yourself and them with more elaborate animations (but elaborate transitions are rarely a good idea, ever). However, in a purely factual and no nonsense presentation to board members for example, animations and transitions should be minimal, if used at all.

To summarise animations and transitions, avoid randomness, feed text in from the left and only use a few different effects in any one presentation. Avoid letting the time be dictated by the computer the presentation is running off and, while thinking of timings, keep both animations and transitions short and punchy.

Getting ever more into the detail of the presentation, let's now turn our attention to the type of information we are communicating to our audience. We'll start by looking at numbers and the next chapter deals with this subject in the context of how to effectively convey numeric information to an audience.

Is the presentation numbers based?

"The things of this world cannot be made known without a knowledge of mathematics."

Roger Bacon

Like so many things related to presenting to an audience, the subject of presenting them with data has a number of rules and guidelines, which we'll summarise here. Firstly and most fundamentally, whatever data you are presenting, can the audience physically read it? Just because you have lifted all 40 cells of a table out of your report doesn't mean that it should be pasted into a PowerPoint presentation. So the first rule is to make sure the audience can read your chart. As a guide, never use a text size of less than 18 point on screen; if it doesn't fit, remove content as opposed to reducing font size!

While on the subject of legibility, check also that the colour of your data contrasts sufficiently with the colour of the slide or table background. If the colours are too similar, then it will be hard for the audience to read them. This then creates an example of design for design sake – The slide looks good, but you can't read it. Incidentally, did you know that around 8% of adult males are colour blind (and only 0.5% of women)? So in a typical audience of 100 people (male and female), eight men and maybe one woman will be colour blind. The simplest way to present numerical data so that it is legible to as many as possible is to stick to charts that are basically black and white – Function over form.

Secondly, any data you present should be understandable to your audience and a tool that helps here is to convert tables into more visually comprehensible charts.

When presenting concepts that include references to data, it can be useful to make the point using a graph or chart. These visual methods can make the point much more strongly than simply narrating the data. While they can be powerful methods, they also have the potential to ruin a presentation if they convey the wrong message, incorrectly emphasize a point or they confuse the audience. Appropriate use of graphs and tables is one way to enhance the message you are delivering.

There are any number of charts available within PowerPoint and here is a selection of guidelines as to the types on offer. Firstly, there are column charts and in these, categories are typically organized along the horizontal axis and values along the vertical axis. Column charts are useful for showing data changes over a period of time or for illustrating comparisons among items.

Next, there are line charts, which can be used to display continuous data over time and are great for showing trends in data at equal intervals. In a line chart, category data is distributed evenly along the horizontal axis, and all value data is distributed along the vertical axis.

Pie charts show the size of items in one data series, proportional to the sum of the overall item. The data points in a pie chart are displayed as a percentage of the whole pie.

Data that is arranged in columns or rows on a worksheet can be plotted in a bar chart. Bar charts illustrate comparisons among individual items.

Area charts emphasize the scale of change over time, and can be used to emphasize the total value across a trend. For example, data that represent sales over time can be plotted in an area chart to emphasize the total sales. By displaying the sum of the plotted values, an area chart also shows the relationship of parts to a whole.

Scatter charts show the relationships among the numeric values in several data series, or plots two groups of numbers as one series of coordinates. A scatter chart has two value axes, showing one set of numeric data along the horizontal axis (x-axis) and another along the vertical axis (y-axis). It combines these values into single data points and displays them in irregular intervals, or clusters. Scatter charts are normally used for displaying and comparing numeric values, such as scientific, statistical, and engineering data.

You may also consider surface charts, which are useful when you want to find optimum combinations between two sets of data. Doughnut charts are hard to read and so should be avoided in most cases. There are plenty of others available too, but here we've covered the most widely used (in presentations) forms of chart.

As you decide which types of charts you think are most effective for presenting your data, remember that a chart or graph is a pictorial interpretation of data. So for the most part you will create a spreadsheet that holds or calculates some type of data, and then use the chart to illustrate said data.

Some of the effects you can apply to your charts may distract or confuse your audience. For example, using 3D on a bar chart makes it harder to define whether the peak of the bar is the front or back of the bar, particularly if there are small differences in the overall values of bars. So the rule of thumb here is to play around with chart types, styles and formats in Excel before deciding which are best for your PowerPoint needs. Once you have a small selection of styles you like, use them consistently in your presentations. By this we mean, if you always use a line chart to show trends over time, don't suddenly introduce a bar chart to show the same type of information.

In summary, when presenting your audience with numerical data, make sure it is big enough for them to read and clear enough for them to understand. Embrace the opportunities offered by charts for visually enhancing the way you present numerical data, but have a clear structure as to what types of charts you use for which forms of data. Develop your own preferred chart (graph) templates that you can quickly and easily drop into presentations. Finally, and above all else, remember that a chart or graph is a pictorial interpretation of data; your aim being to visually convey numerical data in a way that the audience understands and absorbs.

Having dealt with conveying numeric information, let's now move on to words. The next chapter discusses some best and worst practices for presenting text-based information to your audience.

Presenting text-based information

"When words are scarce they are seldom spent in vain."
William Shakespeare

Most presentations are designed with the intent that they will convey information to an audience. It is hoped that as a result the audience will learn and understand the information communicated. But what happens when the presenter tries to convey too much information? Particularly if it is text based? The audience will disengage, become confused and switch off. Simply put, their brains can't keep up with the amount of data coming in and they are unable to process it.

This overload often happens when the presenter has built too much information into their slides. You know the sort of thing, long lists of bullet points or worse still, entire paragraphs of text. The result is that the audience reads the screen content at one speed while the presenter reads it out loud at another (significantly slower). As a result, their working memories become overloaded and so partially shut down. As a presenter, that is not the desired outcome.

Let's look at how we can create slides that are more mentally manageable for an audience to comprehend and take on board. Firstly, let's start with a bold aim – No more than six words on a screen. Although this isn't always possible, it is a good target to aim for. If you need more words, then should or could you split them into two slides? Remember, a slide can be as quickly used as a single frame in a movie and doesn't have to be full of 'stuff' to be effective.

When you have decided which words can remain on screen and you have a clear reason for putting them there, consider their physical appearance. To begin with, they need to be big enough for the audience to read (18 point minimum). Then there is the font or style to select and there are three types to choose from: Serif (one that has serifs or the extra tails on the end of each letter), sans-serif (a font which does not have the serifs or extra bits at the ends of the letters) and script (which looks like handwriting).

When selecting the style of font to use, the easiest to read are sans-serif ones (Arial or Helvetica, for example). Research shows that serif fonts are harder to read when projected onto a screen, so only use these if you really must and the same can be said for scripts.

A second challenging objective to set yourself is to endeavour not to utter any word that is on the screen. Aim for the screen to be the emphasis and visual anchor of the words you are saying. The words on the screen should never, ever be there purely as an *aide-mémoire* for the presenter. That is what the notes pages in PowerPoint and systematic rehearsal are for.

When you are designing your slides, it is fine to storyboard with text and then even to put the text that you will say on the screen. The key differentiations for a Power Presenter are that they then remove the text and place it in the notes section if used anywhere. They also replace the text with visual imagery that makes the same point. For example, and using TV weather presenters again, they could put on the screen that strong winds are sweeping across from west to east.

But instead they tend to say those words and at the same time, the screen shows some arrows moving quickly from the left of the map behind them to the right. They clearly have a message to convey and do so by verbalising it while at the same time making the point visually on screen.

Now here's a point to consider when deciding which words you will have on the screen (ideally a maximum of six). In the UK, up to 16 million adults, nearly half the workforce, are holding down jobs despite having the reading and writing skills expected of children leaving primary school. So keep any words simple. In the USA, the average US newspaper is aimed at 14-year olds in terms of reading age. Some presenters feel an urge to demonstrate their intelligence by using long words on screen. We advise against this for the reasons just given.

There will be some of you reading this that are insistent that you must have lots and lots of words on the screen (and on occasions, that may be true). However, if that really is the case, is a presentation the most suitable format for the information to be conveyed in? Perhaps a report, book or even email would be better. The purpose of this section is to encourage you to think about the words on the screen more from an audience perspective and less from the standpoint of being a crutch for the presenter.

Here are a few more pointers to consider when using text in presentations. All CAPITAL letters together are perceived as the message being shouted (often angrily). Underlining used to be ok for highlighting, but with the Internet it is now associated more with hyperlinks and so can confuse. A more effective way of highlighting a particular word is to change the colour of the text or the background behind it. One more thing, PowerPoint has an inbuilt text design tool Word Art. Unless you are an experienced graphic designer, the best advice is to simply not use it, ever, as many of these effects end up looking amateur and do nothing to enhance the slide.

In summary, when you craft new slides and want to communicate textual information, there are a number of considerations. Firstly, aim for no more than six words on the screen. Secondly, any words that are on the screen should not be said by the presenter; and thirdly, remember that many, many adults literally have the reading ages of children. Oh, and make sure that the style of font you adopt is legible for the audience.

Finally, just because PowerPoint offers such a wide range of ways and techniques you can use to enhance, distort and animate text, doesn't necessarily mean that it's a good thing; only that all these things are *doable*.

If you insist on having words on the screen, then read the next chapter as it contains another sobering thought. We explain why it is that you as a presenter and the audience can and will mentally process the words on screen at different speeds, which leads to them getting ahead of you.

They can read faster than you

"Communication – the human connection – is the key to personal and career success."
Paul J.Meyer

Ok, so you want to put words onto the PowerPoint screen. No problem, but there are a couple of things you should consider as you craft your presentation design. Firstly and most fundamentally, the audience can read faster than you, the presenter, will be speaking and so why would you ever, ever want to put sentences on the screen (i.e. bullet points and the like) and then to read them out slowly and clearly. Acknowledged best practice here is to have no more than six words on the screen. There is a good joke regarding the presenter standing in front of a PowerPoint screen loaded with text and pronouncing to the audience that although he could have emailed the information to each of them, he preferred to read out:

Every... single... word... At... a... most... annoyingly... slow... and... deliberate... pace...

When it comes to the science, people read (silently) around 160 to 170 words per minute. But when talking, we utter between 125 and 150 words per minute. The fact is that the audience can read faster than the presenter is presenting (i.e. talking) and as a result, they'll be taking in information (visually) at a different rate to what it is being aurally delivered and so significantly reducing delivery effectiveness and its embedding into memory.

Secondly in this section, while looking at how humans read, it's worth taking note of the following: Humans read via pattern and shape, this is the same reason why words in all capitals take longer to read. When a word is randomized but the high characters and low characters are fairly close to the same place it is easy enough to read, but if that displacement becomes too large it becomes very difficult, even if the first and last letters are the same. The addition of the first/last letters rule makes it much easier to read, but it is not the true reason why we are able to read it so easily.

Your eyes sort of break the words up into sections based on the tall sections. Here's a good example: *"Adoccrnig to a rhsceearch at Cdbmarige Utinervisy."* As you scan the first word of the phrase if you see a 'd' around the middle you assume it is 'according' and move on. With the 'd' at the beginning it isn't until you reach the end of the word that you can decide what it is, as you have seen no familiar sections, so you are forced to go back and re-evaluate once you have already read it once. The first/last allows you to fairly simply discern the word at that point, but reading every word twice will slow you down significantly. Try reading this entire paragraph: *"Aoccdrnig to a rscheearch at Cmabrigde Uinervtisy, it deosn't mttaer in waht oredr the ltteers in a wrod are, the olny iprmoetnt tihng is taht the frist and lsat ltteer be at the rghit pclae. The rset can be a total mses and you can sitll raed it wouthit a porblem. Tihs is bcuseae the huamn mnid deos not raed ervey lteter by istlef, but the wrod as a wlohe. Amzanig huh?"*

Hopefully we've established that as a general rule, putting any more than just a few words on the screen is detrimental to your presentation. And the way you illustrate those words also impacts on how effectively they will enter the minds and memories of the audience.

In summary, the human brain receives a word via the eyes or ears and then has to convert it into internal representations. After doing this, it then contextualises and understands the meaning. If the word comes from the eyes, then only some of the letters have to be analysed to identify what the word is (see earlier comments). Conversely, if the word is heard, then the recipient needs to convert all of what is heard into an internal representation to construct and so the processing is slower. The message here is to use words on the screen with caution. For the most part they are ineffective and in some cases detrimental to a Power Presentation. For sure, some readers will be very resistant to this and if you really believe that you have to have lots and lots of words on the screen, then ask yourself this question: Is a presentation really the best way to impart this information to others? Perhaps you would be better writing and distributing it as a report. And this leads us nicely on to the contents of the next chapter: What are you producing and delivering to your audience, and in what form(s)?

Presentations and handouts are different things

"The two words 'information' and 'communication' are often used interchangeably, but they signify quite different things. Information is giving out; communication is getting through."
Sydney J. Harris

The title of this chapter may seem somewhat obvious, but you'd be surprised by just how many presenters think that they can distribute their presentation as printed or electronic material to the audience after the event. The point is that if the presentation has been crafted using some of the techniques mentioned elsewhere in this book, then it won't be as effective as it should be in terms of being a handout. For starters, it should lack sufficient text to explain the meaning of each slide, as this is the job of the Power Presenter. Then there is the fact that many animations don't look that good when printed out (although you can if an advanced user of PowerPoint locate items that animate off screen if you don't want to print them).

So, the part of a presentation that is on the screen is the visual medium that works hand in hand with the presenter to deliver multi-sensory messaging in an effective and engaging manner. A handout is somewhat different – It is more an *aide-mémoire* as to what was presented, both visually and spoken. In simple terms, a handout is the presentation including word- and numbers-based annotation that replaces the part of the speaker. Too often, what happens is that the presenter thinks that their job is finished as soon as they leave the stage. They then tend to treat the presentation as surplus to requirements, when in actual fact the handout is the means by which the audience will relate to the presentation at a later date.

Creating an effective post-presentation tool that emphasises the key messages from the presentation is a powerful way to maintain a connection with the audience. Rarely is this achieved by simply distributing two, six or even eight slides per page handouts. This is just a time-saving means of giving the audience something to take away, with little or no regard as to what its purpose is. In actual fact, a good presentation benefits from having an accompanying handout as support because the audience member can more accurately recall the content and context in detail at a later date.

At this point people often complain that they have neither the time nor inclination to create two different presentation formats (presentation and handout). But there is an effective means of creating both with only a minimal of extra effort. The key is to begin by creating the presentation as you normally would including putting text and bullet points on the screen (don't worry, they aren't going to stay there). Then once the presentation is built and all the text explains what is going on upon each slide and acts as a script for the presentation, what you have is a handout in effect. Now all that you have to do to convert this into a much more effective presentation is to cut as much as is physically possible of the text and numeric data from the slide and to paste it into the notes section (see PowerPoint > Views). The result is that you have created a more engaging presentation without those annoying words and numbers that you recite verbatim. Importantly, you've also created a handout that both reminds audience members of the content and is annotated with the detail orated by the presenter at the original event.

Another point to make regarding the differences between handouts and presentation relates to the size, legibility and even orientation of each. What is legible on a great big screen in an auditorium may not be so on a notes page of a multi-slide handout reduced down to A4 in size. So you may need to look at your handouts and adjust them accordingly.

However, don't let the design of the handout over-influence the design and therefore effectiveness of the main event – the presentation. The handout has an important role to play, but it is different to the presentation (as we've already explained).

Another consideration with regard to handouts is that often they are printed in black and white to save ink toner. Why would you go to the time and effort of creating and using colours that enhance your presentation only to take them away from the post-presentation material. If colour is needed, then it is needed and that's it. There is plenty of research out there that demonstrates how integral colour is to what people associate with different company logos and the like. Perceptions almost always change if you change the colour of something.

Nowadays, most people in the developed world have access to a computer, so you can provide them with electronic handouts. These can be the presentation as it appeared on the screen, but also requires annotation or another means of explaining the content to the viewer without cluttering the screen. Another tool you can use here is voice recording a narration. PowerPoint allows you to create an audio file and insert it into each slide in the presentation, then as long as the people you give electronic versions to have speakers on their PCs they will be able to hear your narration. It can be inserted either to play as soon as the slide opens (automatically) or upon a mouse click. A simple but important point to make here is that you need to let those that have the electronic versions know that it has sound and therefore, they need to turn on their speakers to be able to hear it. Otherwise they may just go through the whole thing in silence and so miss the effectiveness and key messages.

To summarise the difference between a presentation and a handout, the former is a combined visual and audio communication of information and key messages. The latter is a means by which a person or persons can review the event at a later date without the need for the presenter being there but to still be able to take on board all the information originally imparted. A handout is not just a calling card that the presenter gives away at the end of the event. It can be, but this significantly dilutes the post event perceptions of the presentation and key information.

Let us return to the headline topic of presentations and specifically related to words and text; the next chapter provides direction and advice relating to the use of bullet points, or as you'll discover the overwhelming benefits of not using them.

Bullets – No, no, no

"Since we can't read and listen at the same time, your audience can only read your bullet points or listen to you (as you present). They can't do both."

Phillip Adcock

In this next chapter, our aim is simple – to persuade readers just how inappropriate bullet points are in almost any presentation. We'd like to demonstrate, using evidence and expert opinion, how bad and inappropriate those apparently innocuous, but so easy and convenient to use, bullet points are.

Behind all the excuses and reasoning often given by those who use bullet points is the hard and cold fact that in truth, bullets are often nothing more than *aides-mémoire* for them as they present. We'd like to challenge readers to think that if bullets are necessary, should they really be a presentation or part of something in another format, such as a report or handout?

Death by bullet point is the most typical, and most predictable, slide format for presenters short on imagination and anything vaguely visually interesting. Over the course of a lengthy presentation (or even a short one for that matter), having one slide after another looking exactly the same can have a hypnotic effect on an audience – a sleepy, hypnotic effect, that is.

The problems with a bullet point-laden slide are (this is a book – bullet points are allowed):

- As soon as you put up the slide, your audience will start reading it – from left to right, top to bottom.

- Which means that they won't be listening to you, the presenter, as you talk about even the first item.

- Since reading is faster than talking, your audience will have finished reading the slide before you're anywhere near talking about it.

- This means that they won't be listening to your commentary as they already know what's coming.

In other words, the bullet point-laden slide is an entirely ineffective way to deliver your message. About the only way you could make it even worse would be by putting even more words on the slide and then read them out word-for-word. Unfortunately, this is still happening in too many presentation venues around the world each and every day.

Garr Reynolds in his blog, *Presentation Zen*, says the following: *"People often ask me how many bullet points is enough for their presentation. My answer is always the same: as few as possible... how about zero? In general, the more bullets your PowerPoint has, the less effective your presentation will likely be."*

At this point, some of you defensive types might be thinking that PowerPoint and other presentation software will let you uncover bullet points incrementally, one at a time, so at least the audience won't be able to read ahead. And although this is true and it's a bit better than uncovering everything at once, this is only really a workaround (which also gets in your way when you have to move back and forth through your slides, e.g. during questions and answers).

If you have a lot to say, how do you avoid bullets? Well let's explore what a bullet pointed list actually is – It's a list. There's nothing wrong with a list as long as the presentation designer recognises that to the audience it's only a list. There are no ideas to mentally process or concepts to decode and think through.

So what can we do to reduce the reliance on bulleted lists in our presentations? Firstly, learn the content so that you as a presenter don't need the script. If you do feel the need to be scripted, then hide it from the audience in the notes section. Another easy way to improve the appearance and effectiveness of a list is to split it into just one line per slide – break up those ten bullets into ten slides. Add relevant, powerful photographs, charts or other visual imagery. If you insist on having the list all together somewhere, re-collate each point into a summary; then you can put them all on the 11th slide. At least by then, the audience will be somewhat familiar with the subject matter.

When thinking further about bullet points, we are indebted to Cliff Atkinson who published an excellent piece in April, 2003, titled *Bullet Points Kill (Effective Communication).* In it he writes: *"Guns don't kill communication. Bullet points kill communication. And when you use bullet points in a PowerPoint, you're shooting yourself in the foot."*

Why do people use bullets? Bullet points do a great job of taking lots of text and turning it into less text. Given a choice between reading a 120-page business plan or a 12-page bullet point summary, most would choose the bullet points.

When it comes to presentations, the problem is that bullet points are the right answer to the wrong question. If the question is, "How do I condense 120 pages of text down to 12 pages of text?" then bullet points are the right answer. But in a visual presentation environment, that's the wrong question. The right question is, "How can I distil my complex information into a visual form that will help me communicate more effectively?" You can begin asking the right question with a simple shift of orientation in your thinking.

So in summary, on the subject of bullet points, firstly, they are never ever to be used as a script or even *aides-mémoire* for you the Power Presenter. Secondly, if you must have lots of words on the screen, is it really a presentation, or alternatively a report? Thirdly, a single title on the screen is more mentally *processable,* so if you have a list that you insist on presenting, split it into just one point per slide and then use impactive visual imagery and graphics to enhance your message. Finally, heed the words of communications expert Cliff Atkinson and think how can you distil your complex information into a visual form that will help you communicate more effectively with your audience?

Or as comedian Don McMillan put it in a single on-screen bullet point:

1) *People tend to put every word they are going to say on their PowerPoint slides. Although this eliminates them needing to*

memorise their patter, ultimately this makes the slides look crowded, wordy and boring. As a result presenters will lose their audience's attention even before they reach the bottom of their...

1) *(Continued)...first slide!*

It isn't only bullet points that are responsible for the ruination of so many good presentations and the devaluing of the information they contain. There's another visual device that's used too often and for the most part inappropriately – clip art. In the next chapter, we'll explore what it is, where it came from and why it is for the most part to be avoided when creating presentations.

Clip Art – No, no, no

"Without tradition, art is a flock of sheep without a shepherd. Without innovation, it is a corpse."
Winston Churchill

Just as bullet points have mistakenly become an essential crutch for far too many PowerPoint presenters nowadays, so has the use of clip art. In this chapter we'll explore the dos and don'ts of using these all-too-often-used crass little cartoon images.

The term clip art is defined as ready-made pieces of printed or computerized graphic art, such as illustrations, borders, and backgrounds, which can be electronically copied and used to decorate (or should that be deteriorate) a presentation or document. The term clip art comes from the books of graphic images once used as a graphics source. Users would cut out or clip the desired artwork from the book to place into layouts. Later, it was common to scan the images from the books.

As a general rule of thumb, avoid using PowerPoint Clip Art or other cartoonish line art. Think of it this way; if it is included in the software, the audience has seen it a million times before. It may have been interesting once, but today the inclusion of such clip art often undermines the professionalism of the presenter and the content of the presentation. Like all things presentation related, there are exceptions to the rule, but think hard and think twice before inserting clip art into your presentation.

In truth, most clip art is just a throwback to a time before so much stunning visual imagery was available on the Internet. In those days, presenters were forced to choose from a pitifully limited array of visual images often supplied on a single CD-ROM. Nowadays, there are more and better visual solutions for presenters to use. For example, images of people inserted into slides are often effective because photography of people tends to help the audience connect with the slide on a more emotional level (see mirror neurons earlier in this book).

We would recommend that Power Presenters take time to learn another software package alongside PowerPoint (or whatever presentation software they choose). Photoshop is good but expensive for creating static visual images that can be the most professional looking. There is a cheaper, simpler-to-use version called Photoshop Elements. Both of these packages allow users to easily manipulate visual images before inserting them into PowerPoint. The makers of Photoshop also have Premiere and Premiere Elements for those that wish to manipulate video and audio for use in presentations (amongst other things).

Once again, if you want to look for a steer in terms of whether to use clip art, take a look at the professional media organisations, such as TV stations, newspapers and magazines. I'll guess you'll find it pretty near impossible to find much clip art in what they are doing. Yet they are recognised masters in visual communication. Need we say more?

As has already been stated, clip art is a throwback to a bygone age; a time before the Internet and such search options as *Google Images*. So unless you want your presentation to have the look and feel of a 1980's self-help seminar, then avoid using it. In any case, more often than not, the images available online are just so much more appropriate than having to shoehorn some crappy little cartoon into your multi-million dollar company trading statement presentation.

In the last chapters, we've pretty much ruled out bullet points and now have definitely ruled out almost all known clip art. Are some of you now worrying that all you have left is a plain blank slide and perhaps a Microsoft PowerPoint template design? Please don't even go there! Hopefully, all we are doing here on our journey though effective presentations is quantifying what works and what doesn't and then offering Power Presenters a more powerful set of tools with which to present (ergo, communicate) with.

Sourcing better graphics

"A picture is worth a thousand words."
Napoleon Bonaparte

We have all sat through PowerPoint presentations where the same graphics seem to be used continuously. These tend to have come from the dreaded clip art library; whilst these images are free and readily available, the question has to be asked, "Do they enhance the presentation?" For reasons just outlined, the answer is a definite NO! Inserting clip art is used as a way of showing the audience that you know how to use certain features of PowerPoint, but does little to enhance the presentation.

To become a Power Presenter you need to think away from this need to use standard clip art images to enhance a presentation. Sources of high quality imagery are available on the Internet either as paid sources or as free. A particular favourite is shutterstock.com; they have a selection of tariffs available depending on the frequency of access to downloading images. In the book *Presentation Zen*, author

Garr Reynold's preferred source of imagery is istockphoto.com. This particular website works on the basis of credits, which is ideal for the occasional user of images. A third supplier is gettyimages.co.uk; once registered, the large array of imagery is available. All of these websites have access to a vast library of quality images, which means there is no excuse for poor graphics in your PowerPoint presentations.

If you still want to access images but without the added cost factor, then try websites such as *Flickr.com* or *Google Images*. Due to the open nature of these sites it may take a little longer to find the right image for your presentation. You will also need to check the copyright associated with each image. Finding the right image may not be the end of the trail; if copyright is applied, you may be guided to one of the sites mentioned above to purchase the desired image.

As you may be working for a large corporate company then a certain restriction on graphics may be enforced, designed to keep brands strong within the market place. These corporate graphics can be a restriction though, especially if a set PowerPoint theme has to be applied. This restriction can cause a diversion from the key message, as company logos appear on every slide. In an ideal situation your company logo need only appear on the first and last slide. Marketing departments should have access to quality images that may mean you not trawling through the websites mentioned above. If you know the image you want then ask for it.

So in summary, whenever you use a graphic it must say something meaningful within the presentation. Remember a quality image can be worth a thousand words and carry a greater impact to the audience. The use of imagery is not the same as inserting a small piece of clip art from the supplied library. If anything, avoid going to the 'Insert' icon followed by the 'Clip Art' icon in PowerPoint. Use quality graphics to present with power and purpose.

So enough about still images, what about moving ones? In the next chapter we look at the use of video clips in presentations and offer some practical advice.

Video dos and don'ts

"Never confuse movement with action."
Ernest Hemingway

In this next chapter, we'll take a look at the use of video as part of presenting to an audience. As technology has advanced, the use of this medium has exploded, and like all things related to presenting, not always for the better.

Here, we are going to address the pros and cons of using the current PowerPoint enhancement of inserting video and will offer a basic guide as to how and how not to use it. For example, what is the purpose of a video clip? Is that the best option? And why not just insert it because either the ad agency provided it or it happens to exist? Too many presenters seem to think that just because they have access to some video clip or other, then they are compelled to shoehorn it into their presentation, but why? Often, nowadays, the presenter will stand up and begin their presentation with something like, "I'd like to start with playing you this…" Next time you are witness to such an event, pay particular attention to the presenter themselves as the clip plays. Often they'll begin by looking intently at the screen and the clip playing, and then they start to shuffle or fidget as if they are receiving a group telepathic message from the audience that questions the relevance, duration, etc.

Videos are a great way to enhance presentations; for example, you can use *vox pop* and clips of others talking to reinforce your messages. Another good use is to use them to keep the audience interested by presenting them with the occasional (but relevant) video surprise.

However, there are a number of considerations that we need to make before blindly inserting video clips into presentations. Firstly and fundamentally, we need to make sure that the audience has been cued up with regard to what to expect from the clip, and this means making sure that we explain sufficiently about the content and context. Secondly, give serious thought to the length of any clip used. Although the human race can sit through a 90-minute movie completely absorbed in the plot, try showing more than a couple of minutes in a presentation context and for the most part you are pushing your luck.

As another rule of thumb, video clips used in presentations need to be short, punchy and 'in your face' relevant. Subtlety is for other forms of communication. Looking at these factors individually, videos need to be short enough to hold the attention of the audience, but long enough to make sense. A good place to learn how to do this is to watch how expertly advertising agencies make use of 30-second commercial slots within ad breaks on TV. With regard to video clips being long enough, the presenter (you), the preceding content, or the clip itself has to provide the context to go with the video message. By way of an example of how not to do it, at a recent retail convention a speaker began by showing the assembled audience of supply chain experts a montage of their recent TV adverts. The audience wanted to know about technology and systems, the speaker began by presenting a video relating to selling groceries to shoppers – Irrelevant, disengaging and pointless. But this did get the advertising agency a mention, so no doubt they thought it a worthwhile exercise.

It is also recommended that you check and double check that your video clip is in fact relevant to what you are presenting about. This often means testing it on others. Although you know all about the video and why you've chosen it, is it really obvious to others?

This isn't a book about the technologies of presenting but it is worth noting here that even now, video is a memory hungry thing for computers to handle. What's more, there are so many different types and formats (not to mention codecs). Our advice is simple: Never stand up on stage without having first checked that your clips play, that they play in the right order, are started by the correct action and that they play all the way through. The more the venue managers or presentation agency assure you that all will be alright on the night, the more you should absolutely insist on checking that each clip plays as it should. We've seen clips not even start (and then the presenter goes delving around their computer documents directory in full view of the audience, trying to locate the mischievous clip). Sometimes clips stop prematurely and we've even seen completely the wrong clip begin to play; after an innocuous click of the mouse, what should have been a clip of people shopping was replaced with some seriously hard core pornography.

In summary, video clips can be a great asset to Power Presenters, but their use needs to be tempered and sense checked. Are they necessary? Do they add anything to the presentation? And do they work as they are supposed to? Also, when you are rehearsing your presentation, be mindful of what you should do as a clip is playing as, chances are, you want the audience to keep their attention on the clip, not focussing on you playing pocket billiards at the side of the stage.

Finally on the subject of video clips, there are many different video editing packages available, some are free to download and others cost upwards of £1,000. If you use one of these or are tempted, then they can significantly enhance the quality of your video clips. You can zoom in, speed up, freeze frame, and add text and a host of other effects. You can create montages of clips, add music or narration and even play the clips backwards. But like we've said a few times, before diving into the special effects bin, just make sure that what you are creating is appropriate for what you are presenting. Just like all those slide transitions in PowerPoint, special effects in video can be at least distracting and at worst downright annoying.

Let's now move onto the audio side of a presentation and in the next chapter, we'll explore the possible use of all things sound related.

Music & sounds

"After silence, that which comes nearest to expressing the inexpressible is music."

Aldous Huxley

Although visual is the predominate sense used in connection with receiving a PowerPoint presentation, second is audio and within it comes music and sounds. In this chapter, we'll explore various options to do with sound. Firstly, how to pick music styles, genres etc. Then we'll touch on other sounds available such as rounds of applause, laughter and those inane clicks and dings.

With regard to any music or sound, it is again a case of what it will bring to the presentation. Does it enhance or detract from the key messages? In many cases, sounds can be thought of as being like audio clip art. In summary, what we're going do to now is audit the audio!

Firstly, let's cover the playing of any sounds. Many laptops are used to deliver presentations to audiences large and small, but for the most part they have an inbuilt limitation and that is the quality of their speakers. Even if you are only presenting to a couple of people, if sound forms part of your presentation, then try to broadcast it through something other than the inbuilt laptop speakers. There are some very good compact speakers available for just a few pounds, and they are only the size of the typical computer mouse.

Turning to the subject of music, once you decide that you want to use it to enhance your presentation, just check it meets these three criteria as a first off: The style and genre is suitable for the tone and content of the presentation; it is also appropriate for the audience you are presenting to; and finally, it is of an acceptable quality to broadcast. With these three boxes ticked, you can then decide how long you want the music to last. For example, is it an intro, an outro or just a filling of some description? Whatever it is to be used for, make sure that there is something else happening at the same time, as you don't want your audience to be just listening to your music, with their other four senses dormant and free to mentally wander. Try if you can to have the music fade in and out if possible; this sounds more professional than it just jumping in and out. Once again, there is any number of audio editing software packages available at a wide variety of price points. Basically, for music in a presentation all you need to do is manage the length of the clip and adjust the volume at different points as it plays (entry, exit and if you want to speak over parts).

Similar criteria also apply to spoken word audio, as it does to music. However, with this type of sound, you may also want to consider the speed at which it is spoken and try to avoid strong local accents that the audience may struggle with. If you are familiar with a video editing package, then you may be able to overlay some audio with sub-titles if you need to enhance its clarity.

Now let's move on to other sorts of sounds you can incorporate into your presentations. As a guide, try to avoid those annoying audio clip art sounds such as dings, clicks and swishes that accompany any slide builds, animations and transitions. If you are presenting your key messages, check that any accompanying sounds are appropriate, as many clip art-related types are somewhat cartoony and not in keeping with Power Presenting. When you do use sounds, they need to either work in the background (such as a sound effect on the radio) or be long enough to make sense. For example, any sound must be long enough and clear enough to be comprehensible to your audience.

One form of sound that has become popular is extracts from TV and the movies (often termed movie WAVs) – These can be effective if prudently used, but just check any copyright restrictions, especially if you intend to distribute your presentation in any way. But if used creatively, these little sound bites are a great way to generate emotional engagement to the messages you are presenting.

There is one other form of sound worth commenting on and that is the sound of you, the presenter. If you are miked up then that helps with the delivery (but remember that the mike may be on when you aren't on stage!). Be mindful of other sounds you may be inadvertently making such as rattling change in your pockets or walking around the stage in squeaky shoes. Like all things presentation related, a lot comes down to attention to detail. I would go as far as to say that conduct your own dress rehearsal prior to delivering your final Power Presentation, during which you can check for unwanted audio-related distractions.

One final point to make on this subject is to do with actually triggering sounds to play. Depending on your computer skills, try not to overcomplicate sound deployment, for example expecting sounds to perfectly accompany some visual animation on screen. Different computers have different processing powers and quite often, what plays in perfectly choreographed harmony on one machine is out of sync on another. A safer option is to have the sounds playing before or after any other animation so that small timing gaps aren't critical. The same rules apply when using multiple audio clips. Try to avoid having them independently play together or in a tightly choreographed sequence. Either create a single audio file in an audio editing package or have the sounds each independently play one at a time.

In summary, adding sound to your presentation can be a great way to add depth and emotion to the content, but as is becoming a recurring message, use sound wisely. Make sure any music is suitable for the audience and appropriate for the presentation content. Avoid introducing a music track just because you happen to like it. With regard to other audio options, avoid audio clip art as a rule of thumb and make sure any sound bites are loud enough and clear enough for the audience to hear them.

In the last few chapters, we've talked of using different aspects to build an absolutely brilliant presentation, but before leaving the subject, there's one other topic that we feel is worthy of discussion here. In the next chapter we'll offer advice and recommendations regarding what to do if the presentation you are to deliver isn't something that you created (belongs to someone else).

Owning someone else's presentation

"Taking something from one man and making it worse is plagiarism."
George A. Moore

The concept of using somebody else's presentation is not unusual. Corporate organisations can issue presentations across a group, which allows for a consistent brand to be promoted. A global company may require consistency across sales presentations. Alternatively, colleagues may simply fall ill and you are asked to present on their behalf. Whichever of these situations you are faced with careful thought ought to be given to how you will be presenting.

When presented with someone else's presentation you need to make it your own. In essence you need to own the presentation, live it and believe in it. Any frailty will be picked up by the audience.

So how do you own a presentation you don't actually own?

Several steps need to be applied, in the first instance these can be:

1. Changing the slides.

2. Changing the narrative.

3. Practising.

Follow these three steps to start the ownership process:

<u>Changing the slides</u>

If you are presented with a corporate presentation then there may be a limit to what you are allowed to edit with regard to content. The least you would expect is to add your name to the presentation as an introductory page. The essence of owning a presentation is to make it personal to you, retelling a past story that is relevant to the topic in the presentation relaxes not only yourself but also welcomes the audience into your world. If the option is available add in a few extra slides that reinforce the key message; this is essential if you are faced with a presentation with bullet points. If this is the case, remember not to use the bullet points as a script, the audience can read quicker than the spoken word, as we keep saying.

Changing the narrative

Many corporate presentations come with a predefined script to support each PowerPoint slide. This is a great starting point with regard to the presentation, as the key messages will be emphasised. It is important though not to simply rely on the supporting text. Care needs to be taken that the script does not simply regurgitate what is going to appear as bullet points. As a Power Presenter you must look at refining the narrative of the presentation, especially if local slang and terminology play a part. Delivering the key message of the presentation will still be possible but as a presenter you will feel more comfortable by making the changes and so owning the presentation.

Practising

There is no better way of owning the presentation then to practise, practise and practise further. Never read through a presentation once and think you can present; it simply will not be a success. There may be occasions when you are thrust into the limelight due to a colleague's illness. If this is the case then hopefully you will have had 24-hours notice. This will allow time to shut the office door and practise; even better, work from home that day to gain the sanctuary required to practise the presentation.

If a colleague does fall ill and you are asked to step into the breach then, apart from owning the presentation, some other aspects need to be considered. Is the presentation you are about to use password protected? If so, who apart from your colleague has the password? During this book several chapters refer to video as an improvement tool. This one example is where having a practice video would benefit those having to step in at the last minute. Just visualising the presentation style of a colleague will allow an understanding to be built up quickly and efficiently. You should still add your own points of emphasis but the visual concept works well. Your colleague will hopefully have a few notes on audience members, for example the key contacts and potential targets as clients. These last few options form one element of becoming a Power Presenter.

Inheriting a presentation from a fellow Power Presenter will mean for an easier transition when inheriting a presentation. Inheriting a PowerPoint presentation full of bullet points needs serious consideration within the confines of the prepared message. Whichever of the situations you are faced with the key is to own the presentation when presenting; adding a little bit of yourself into the presentation will start the connection process with the audience. This will open the mind for the message to be conveyed, but to maximise you must practise, practise and practise some more.

Section 2 – Your Presentation: Summary

"Content makes poor men rich; discontent makes rich men poor."
Benjamin Franklin

As we arrive at the end of Section 2, let's review what we have covered. Firstly, we began by looking at how you can theme and tone your presentation to better match the type of content and information you are communicating. For example, witticisms and humour may be acceptable in a marketing-related presentation, more so than in an event related to paediatric surgery. We also recommended that like all good tales, your presentation should have a beginning, middle and an end. In addition, it should emotionally connect with an audience in a way that takes them on an emotional journey slide by slide.

In the next chapter we asked the fundamental question of what message the presentation is conveying. We recommended that presenters should have identified and have in mind a message or messages they are intent on conveying before they start designing their slides and the detail of the presentation. The book then went on to ask further questions of anyone preparing to design a presentation. What is the one question that the audience wants an answer to? Think about their perspective of the event. For example, why are they attending? Then consider what is most important to them. On the subject, the key learning was that a failure to consider and recognise what the audience wants at a basic level is a sure-fire way to designing an ineffective presentation.

Then the book moved on to look at the matter of time and we explored the ramifications of the fact that the human brain has a maximum attention span of around 20 minutes, so presentations over this timescale have the danger of key messages getting lost as the audience reaches its collective boredom threshold. On the subject of boredom thresholds and the human brain, we then looked at how the audience would remember your presentation and how they had to utilise their short and long term memories, each of which perform very differently. We then revealed that as soon as your short term working memory has finished with its involvement in the process, it erases all the data it used while conducting the screen evaluation and moves on to the next immediate task that you need it to undertake. And this deletion happens within around 18 seconds of the information being received. Therefore you need to make sure that your key messages are not only processed and comprehended by the short term memory, but also embedded into long term memory by making sure they are fully understood and tagged with emotion.

At this stage we began focussing in on particular aspects of the presentation itself, starting with the importance of considering how many delegates may be at the presentation venue. This is because the same slide will carry different emphases on a large projected screen in a large auditorium, compared with the same slide shown to a small group of delegates on a plasma screen. This in turn leads on to designing a presentation in relation to how well you know the audience and that if you are presenting to colleagues who know you well, then they already understand and recognise your personality. However, if you are new to your audience, then it is advisable to take a number of steps early in your presentation so as to create the suitable respect and rapport for the messages you are communicating. So in summary, taking into consideration the type or types of people in your audience and their knowledge of you at the design stage of your presentation can be a powerful way of creating the most effective way to deliver your key messages.

We then revealed a key, but often overlooked aspect of human evolution that directly relates to audience attention. The fact that speech has only been part of human communication for a fraction of our evolutionary development. Your audiences are yet to evolve a natural ability to work with this new-fangled communication contraption known as language (spoken or written). This then supports the famous saying that a picture speaks a thousand words. Power Presenters are those who can communicate their messages the most effectively and using evolutionary hard-wiring is a great way of doing this. Humans have yet to fully evolve to naturally use words, language and numbers. Graphs can simplify how you present numeric information so that the audiences can more easily mentally process it. Images used as visual adjectives can be beneficial if you need to get what you are saying to be embedded in the brains of those in the audience.

An integral part of evolution is emotion and unless you have an emotional connection to what you are seeing and hearing, there is little chance of it getting past your short term memory and embedding itself effectively into your long term memory. Understanding and working with the emotions of the audience are absolutely pivotal to all Power Presenters. Thinking of how your presentation will make the audience feel (emotionally) will lead to much more emotionally engaging results. Ergo, more of your key messages will successfully find their way into the long term memories of the audience.

Again, from an evolutionary perspective, we discussed the six key drivers that all humans are motivated by. This offers a great opportunity for presenters to tailor their presentation to cover each of these evolutionary drivers, and then it's highly likely that they will more effectively engage the audience. To recap, the fitness indicators are: General intelligence, openness to experience, conscientiousness, extraversion, agreeableness and emotional stability.

Continuing to look at the detail that makes up a Power Presentation, we then turned our attention to the first slide that the audience sees and the tremendous importance it has. The cover slide can and should offer your audience a name for the presentation and a description of what to expect. Also the first slide should be designed to represent the tone of the presentation and how you want the audience to anticipate what the content will be and the style in which it will be delivered. Power Presenters should take time to think about how the cover slide can manage expectations and pre-presentation perceptions of the audience as well as helping them, themselves to remember the vital first few lines of the patter.

Then we looked at the fact that humans have a limitation with regard to the pace at which they can take information on board. And as a result, Power Presenters need a template for making sure they pace the feed of information at an acceptable level, and that depends on the type of audience. The subject of Cognitive Load Theory explained how to make complex things easy to understand. If you recall, the theory is based on understanding how those trying to learn actually process incoming information to retain it for future use (remember it). Recognise and estimate the cognitive load threshold of the audience and then feed the information to them at an acceptable level. For example, a room full of clinical psychologists will be able to absorb more information about all things psychology related, than the typical audience at one of those inspirational pseudo-psychologically related 'think and grow rich' events.

Next, we discussed a very powerful but somewhat underused presentation technique. The tool is based on a psychological term known as cognitive dissonance, which is defined as a discomfort caused by holding conflicting cognitions (e.g. ideas, beliefs, values, emotional reactions) simultaneously. When on stage, present an audience with information that on the surface doesn't make any sense. Said information can be spoken but is often better presented visually, on screen. This results in the audience being forced to do more mental processing to make sense of what's in front of them. Ergo, their attention is retained and usually increased.

When you develop the skills to use cognitive dissonance well, your presentations will improve significantly. But as with all things presentation related, be careful not to introduce negative cognitive dissonance such as factually incorrect information on screen.

We then reminded readers to be mindful of never expecting the audience to process more than seven bits of information at any one time. A good guide is to look at each slide and to quantify how much information you are expecting the audience to take on board at any one time. If the number is above seven, then seriously consider splitting the content into two or more separate slides.

Another way to manage potential information overload is to let slides build at a manageable rate in front of the audience. A slide that builds in front of an audience as the presenter tells the tale helps the audience to remember something. You hit an audience with too much information too fast and they'll close down and as a result remember next to nothing. Try to pace the rate of information you put on screen, don't overcrowd the screen and be willing to add more and more slides. Try to keep it to a single message per slide and then use the build to develop the message so that it becomes embedded in the brains of the audience.

Most slide builds involve transitions and the book then offered a number of dos and don'ts: Avoid randomness, feed text in from the left and only use a few different effects in any one presentation. Finally, keep both animations and transitions short and punchy.

We then looked at what are and how you should identify the key messages (mentioned in a previous section) of your presentation and then design the output around them. Typically aim for a maximum of seven messages, use them as the agenda or index, section breaks and as the final summary of your presentation. If any of your key messages are numbers based, remember to make sure it is big enough for the audience to read and clear enough for them to understand. When you want to communicate textual information, aim for no more than six words on the screen. Secondly, any words that are on the screen should not be said by the presenter and thirdly, remember that many, many adults literally have the reading ages of children. Oh, and make sure that the style of font you adopt is legible for the audience. On the matter of text, remember that the audience can read faster than the presenter is presenting (i.e. talking) and as a result, they'll be taking in information (visually) at a different rate to what it is being verbally delivered.

Some text is needed, especially when providing the audience with handouts, but remember, presentations and handouts are not the same things. The former is a combined visual and audio communication of information and key messages. The latter is a means by which a person or persons can review the event at a later date without the need for the presenter being there but still able to take on board all the information originally imparted.

Anything text related naturally leads on to the thorny subject of bullet points and our advice is simple (and scientifically substantiated). Bullet points are never ever to be used as a script or even *aides-mémoire* for you the Power Presenter. If you must have lots of words on the screen, is it really a presentation, or alternatively a report? Finally, a single title on the screen is more mentally processable, so if you have a list that you insist on presenting, split it into just one point per slide and then use impactive visual imagery and graphics to enhance your message.

Just as bullet points have mistakenly become an essential crutch for far too many PowerPoint presenters nowadays, so has the use of clip art. As a general rule of thumb, avoid using PowerPoint Clip Art or other cartoonish line art. Think of it this way – If it is included in the software, the audience has seen it a million times before. There are more and better visual solutions for presenters to use. For example, images of people inserted into slides are often effective because photography of people tends to help the audience connect with the slide on a more emotional level (see mirror neurons earlier in this book).

We then showed how video clips can be a great asset to Power Presenters, but their use needs to be tempered and sense checked: Are they necessary, do they add anything to the presentation and do they work as they are supposed to? Adding sound to your presentation can be a great way to add depth and emotion to the content, but as is becoming a recurring message, use sound wisely. Make sure any music is suitable for the audience and appropriate for the presentation content. Avoid introducing a music track just because you happen to like it. With regard to other audio options, avoid audio clip art as a rule of thumb and make sure any sound bites are loud enough and clear enough for the audience to hear them.

In the next section, we're going on to explore what happens when you, the presenter, and your presentation come together – It's show time! This next group of chapters are all about your performance and how you can improve the ways with which you communicate with the audience.

Section 3

Your performance

Section 3 – Your performance: Introduction

"There is no better than adversity. Every defeat, every heartbreak, every loss, contains its own seed, its own lesson on how to improve your performance the next time."
Malcolm X

In the previous sections, we have concentrated very much on you as a presenter in Section 1 and your presentation in Section 2. In this next section, we're going to focus more on your performance. By that we mean, how you do as a presenter combined with the presentation and venue deliver a stunning overall piece of communication? To start with, we'll explore the relevance of how your presentation fits into any bigger series of presentations. For example, you may be providing a 30-minute talk during a three-day conference. We'll cover the matter of where your presentation sits within that day of the audience's lives. And at a more detailed level, when your presentation is part of a larger event, it's always advisable to check for duplication of content or, worse still, direct contradiction. Endeavour to have somebody (perhaps the event organiser) check that the presentations do in fact work together. This same chapter touches on techniques you can use to build rapport with your audience, including referring to other speakers by their Christian name and referencing aspects of content from previous presentations by others.

Just as individual slides make up part of a presentation and should flow from one to another in a logical and understandable order, then so do presentations link together to become an event

It is human nature to fidget and for the mind to drift away from an intended thought process if we are enclosed in a single space for any length of time. The next chapter in this section goes on to investigate the influence that breaks have on delegates. Are they looking forward to the next break or have they just had one and need re-engaging?

As well as discussing aspects of your audience, this chapter also explores how the venue can directly impact on a presentation. For example, the orientation of a room plays an important role in the success of a presentation. If the orientation is right then delegates are more likely to absorb the information coming their way; get the orientation wrong and messages can be lost due to the discomfort experienced by delegates. Also, the configuration and orientation of the room may also be different from the environment that all of your practice took place in.

Another venue-related element to pay attention to is the freedom available at the venue with regard to movement and interaction with the audience. For example, when attending exhibitions with built-in conference areas within the exhibition stands, more often than not a lectern will be in place to the side of the screen. This is a stage design which may portray a sense of imposed knowledge but as a presentation stance lacks any flexibility. This chapter explores not only why, but also offers practical advice regarding making the most of the venue surroundings.

In the next chapter, we look at three specific tools you can use to further introduce professionalism into your presentation delivery. Firstly, we explore what seems to be a basic aspect of presenting – how to stand. Then we add to that by looking at whether you should be still or rove around the stage, or even mix it, in with the audience. Finally in this section, we offer advice so that you come across as engaging with the entire audience more than just standing there and staring out into the auditorium or worse, at your notes on the screen next to you.

Next you'll discover just how effective it can be for you to stand to the left of the screen (as the audience sees it) and how this lets you choreograph information coming onto each slide. This leads on to a subject known as 'dual encoding', which can be defined as a presentation technique that involves concurrent verbal and visual encoding. This technique has been shown to be significantly more powerful than singular verbal or visual encoding in terms of post presentation audience recall of content.

When we're designing and delivering our presentations, we all strive (consciously or sub-consciously) to draw attention to different aspects of what we are saying and visualising on screen. In this next chapter, we look at a number of techniques designed specifically to draw the attention of the audience toward or away from a particular aspect of the presentation.

Next, we look at how you can further refine your presenting style to make sure that even more of your presentation becomes firmly embedded within the brains of your audience. Having established that by forcing the audience to simultaneously process verbal messages and visual imagery disproportionately improves their learning ability, we go on to discuss adding synchronisation to your sensory output. Effective synchronised dual encoding consists of four different components that are then executed in an almost choreographed manner. Each is explored individually.

A great help when you are presenting, and specifically dual encoding information into the minds of your audience, is the humble remote presentation clicker; something you really should seriously consider if you want to deliver a truly memorable, engaging and professional presentation. As a Power Presenter, not only do you need the right presentation but you also need the right tools of the trade. One of these tools is the wireless presentation remote clicker: A small handheld device that gives you direct control of presentation navigation from pretty much anywhere in the room. These devices will be discussed in more detail.

We then go on to take a look at another presenting secret that is used too infrequently. What we're talking about is using silence; specifically between slides within a presentation. For some reason, most presenters think that they have to talk continually during their presentations – Find out why they don't!

We then look in detail at probably the most important aspect of the design and creation of a good presentation. If there is one single thing that will help most of us have the confidence to deliver the best presentation we can, it's having the confidence in our own ability to do so. When we analyse what it is that shakes the confidence of those about to present, a lot comes down to them simply forgetting what to say and going blank. Throughout this book there are a number of tools that can be used to minimise this risk, but in this section we look at how and why you should invest time and effort rehearsing your presentation.

There is another aspect of the presentation to which we all should pay that extra bit of attention and that's what we move on to next, and it revolves around attention to detail. Audiences love errors on screen; they seek them out, they hunt them down and they like nothing more than pointing them out during the actual event. This frustrating aspect of human behaviour does little to benefit the presentation. It hits the confidence of the presenter and undermines the credibility of their content for starters. So the best way to avoid such a situation is to thoroughly check, double check and review the presentation before the big event.

Because it is inevitable that there are some who will forget their lines and who will present incorrect data, we also discuss the implementation of a safety net strategy in the coming pages. We will go beyond just talking of safety nets regarding the presentation; we also consider a backup plan regarding making sure the presentation will function correctly at the venue.

Then we go on to discuss the topic of audience participation. Should it be encouraged, can it be prevented and how is it best handled? What about questions and answers? All this and more is covered in the coming pages.

So just as you as a mortal are a mere speck in time, so too may your presentation be a small component of something much bigger. In the next chapter, we'll discuss numerous aspects to consider in relation to your presentation being part of a bigger event.

Where are you in the big picture?

"The whole is more than the sum of its parts."
Aristotle

Here, we'll look at how your presentation fits into any bigger series of presentations. For example, you may be providing a 30-minute talk during a three-day conference. Alternatively, you may be the only presentation at a particular meeting or event.

The aim here is to offer practical advice regarding how you can optimise your own professionalism, while at the same time develop a meaningful rapport with the audience.

To begin with, consider the mindset of the audience at the start of your presentation: What is it, what caused it and where would you like it to be? Once you recognise these aspects, you can begin to tailor your offering to capture more of their attention. It isn't wise to just blindly launch into your patter without first trying to engage the audience and to do this, it's advisable to identify how engaged or disengaged they are.

Firstly, look at where your presentation sits within that day of the audience's lives. At a fundamental level, when your presentation is part of a larger event, it's always advisable to check for duplication of content or, worse still, direct contradiction. Endeavour to have somebody (perhaps the event organiser) check that the presentations do in fact work together. The impact and effectiveness of an event can be greatly reduced if the speakers deliver contradicting key messages (one of them at least is likely to lose significant credibility).

As well as checking for contradictions, try to avoid you and others saying the same thing, particularly if this involves using the same data sources (unless referenced as complementary), video clips and examples. In summary, your presentation should be unique in itself, but designed to work as an integral part of the event it is integral to.

When it comes to working with any other speakers presenting, the first tool you can use is to reference their key messages in your own presentation. The very act of saying; "as Jim (Smith) said earlier, X, Y and Z", gives the audience the perception that you and Jim know each other and have mutual respect. Incidentally, surveys reveal that people like hearing their own name because it increases rapport and intimacy. Recall how in everyday life when someone says your name, you instantly feel more noticed, useful or special.

If previous and forthcoming speakers are in fact your peers, then there is a subtle technique you can employ that will result in the audience having a higher opinion of you, yourself. It goes something like this – Ask the audience to think of a carbonated drink known as 'the real thing'. Secondly ask them to think of a sports brand related to 'just do it'; and thirdly, think of the person on stage in front of them and associate them with [insert your presentation topic here]. Now inform the audience that these three very different entities all deliver and attend presentations as a core information transference activity. On the surface, you've just made a relatively unimportant comparison, but deeper within the psyches of the audience, they now see you in the same way as they look at two of the most well known commercial organisations on the planet – Instant respect to you!

What about referencing those who will present after you? This again can be used positively if done so correctly. Once you reference any headline to be talked about subsequently by another speaker, you then create an anchor to that topic with you and your presentation. In other words, when the speaker mentions what you said they would talk of, then the audience is mentally reminded of you and your content.

Overall, even though you probably think that your presentation is the most important at the event, your primary aim should be for your key messages to be effectively embedded in the minds of the audience. It is easier for them to remember the big story as opposed to just your detailed chapter.

When it comes to competitive presentation situations (pitches), remember to never criticise your competitors, and here's why. You never know what they or you will do next. Or to put things another way, never step on people as you race by them going up the ladder as you may need them to catch you as you tumble back down again sometime in the future.

In most presentation scenarios, it will be perceived as bad publicity for you if you appear to criticise others. More effective is to focus on the positives and improve your own offering. In other words, help the audience to come to the conclusion that you are better than your competitors rather than you directly telling them.

Earlier, we said that it may be that you are the only presentation at the event; then what should we do differently in this scenario? To begin with, the techniques of referencing others still hold true and you can still build your own persona by referring to your peers, even if they aren't in the room or connected with the event. For example, you could relay an anecdote originally told by someone famous and then attribute it to them, which in turn will link you to them in the minds of the audience.

A significantly different approach when being the only presenter involves managing more of the audience attention mindset. The first thing you need to do is get their attention; it may be that they've just entered the room and are mentally elsewhere. Here are a couple of proven tools for grabbing the attention of a new audience. Firstly, ask one of them a direct question, this will have the effect of making others aware that they may be called upon and so had better pay attention. Secondly, play an impactive multimedia clip that allows the audience time to make the mental transition from out of the room to into the room and paying attention to you (a couple of minutes maximum).

Just as individual slides make up part of a presentation and should flow from one to another in a logical and understandable order, then so do presentations link together to become an event. Whatever the scenario, consider your presentation as part of an overall communication. It may be a large part or a smaller component but, whichever it is, design and deliver it to work effectively in the context in which it will be given.

Particularly at conferences and exhibitions, competitors may be speaking either before or after your own presentation. Whilst you should be completely solid in your beliefs regarding your own presentation, it is still worth considering if it could be more directed to beat a competitor's offering. This is where two important elements need to be considered.

This scenario occurred in several sales presentations undertaken for Local Government. Suppliers were ushered into a meeting to give a presentation about a particular product. Whilst this situation is never ideal it was the framework laid down and suppliers had to conform to stand any chance of winning tenders. These events were usually in open conference rooms with suppliers at different corners of the room, each having a fixed timeframe in which to perform their presentation.

The goal was to understand several key facts:

1. How well do you know your own presentation?

2. How well do you know your own product?

3. How much are you aware of your competitors' products?

4. How much are you aware of your competitors' presentations?

5. What is the presentation style of your competitors?

By now you will be aware of how important it is to know your own presentation. Being able to control the timing of the presentation gives you a real advantage. Without questioning, you should be able to add or remove specific comments from the presentation. Tailoring your message specifically to the audience should be done without any loss of clarity or emphasis. Having this understanding allows competitive changes for key presentations.

If a competitor is presenting, then gather as much information as possible about their presentation:

1. What time do they have available?

2. Are all times comparable?

3. What will be their focus?

4. Who is performing their presentation?

5. Is there a break between presentations?

Gathering this detail of information will allow a picture to be built of how your presentation may evolve.

If equal time is not available for your presentation, it is within your rights to question with the organiser why not? A coffee break overrunning or a pending lunch break should not be accepted reasons. Your time to present your company needs to be conveyed as equally important.

If a break is scheduled to take place between presentations this can be an ideal opportunity to mingle with an audience. By mingling you should be able to understand the core elements that a purchaser is interested in. At the same time, questions that relate to your product can be either answered individually or added to the presentation as a whole. Work on the basis that if one person is asking the question, a number within the audience are bound to be thinking the same question but are afraid to ask.

Having knowledge of any competitive overlap will allow you to slightly change the emphasis of your own presentation. At all times you must believe in your own presentation and your own product. Showing signs of hesitancy, negative body language or nerves during your presentation will send alarm bells ringing within the audience.

Ah, never forget the audience; and in the next chapter, we'll reveal how the very timing of your presentation slot should impact on aspects of your performance. What we're going to talk about is where you are billed to appear in relation to any breaks the delegates may have just had or be in desperate need for.

When was the last break for delegates?

"If a man insisted always on being serious, and never allowed himself a bit of fun and relaxation, he would go mad or become unstable without knowing it."
Herodotus

It is human nature to fidget and for the mind to drift away from an intended thought process if we are enclosed in a single space for too long. In this particular section we will be investigating the influence that breaks have on delegates. Added to that topic is being clear on when to try to avoid or change a particular presentation slot.

The human brain has a short attention span at around 20 minutes (we've said that a number of times before, but because the last time was more than 20 minutes ago...). After this time the brain will start to disconnect from the presentation you are showing, in the majority of cases irrespective of the quality of the presentation. When you are accepting a presentation slot from a conference organiser, one of the first questions you need to ask is: When was the last break for delegates?

This simple question is important. Imagine performing a presentation at 11.30am when the last break for delegates was the 10.15-10.30 coffee break. Straight after your presentation delegates will be going for their 12.00 lunch break. This situation is one that often occurs at conferences. The conference organisers need to squeeze as many presentations into the day so as to justify the cost of the conference for delegates.

The scenario outlined would be a concern to any presenter. Firstly, delegates would be sitting down for an hour before your presentation. Whilst their attention may be with you for a short time the chances are delegates will be fidgety, causing a disturbance in the presentation arena. One or two fidgets in the audience will soon multiply, similar to a Mexican wave at a stadium.

Secondly, your time for the presentation is scheduled for 30 minutes. As mentioned, the optimum time for the brain to concentrate is 20 minutes. Careful consideration therefore has to be given to the content included in the presentation and the most effective time to mention the key message(s).

The final cause for concern when presented with the timeframe in the scenario is the immediate onset of lunch. As stomachs start rumbling, are delegates going to be engaged in a question and answer session? By staying silent delegates may hope for an early finish. So it is now established that presenting at this time is not ideal and should be avoided; let another presenter have the slot. Negotiate with the conference organiser for a more realistic opportunity to present, when your key messages will be converted.

Some opportunities do exist when the audience is fresh. These are when delegates have had the opportunity to walk around and refresh. These opportunities are immediately after delegates have taken a refreshment break. This will also provide the opportunity to mingle ahead of your presentation; an opportunity lost if presenting in the scenario above. Three key presentation slots are available during the day. These are immediately at the start of the conference, immediately after a morning coffee break and immediately after the afternoon coffee break. Notice immediately after the lunch break is not included because as the digestion of lunch starts, an element of drowsiness takes over the delegates. This outcome can only be detrimental to your presentation and so avoid if at all possible.

So with a presentation slot of your choice secured the only remaining question is to settle on the length of the presentation. We have already mentioned that 20 minutes is an ideal. This length of presentation falls into the concentration scope for the brain. It also provides the opportunity to build a presentation with an introduction before hitting the delegates with the key messages and then tailing the presentation off ready for any questions and answers.

In summary then, don't just accept the first presentation slot offered to you by a conference organiser. When accepting an invitation to present, be fully aware of when delegates had their last break. Presenting when delegates have being sitting down for an hour is not conducive to a successful presentation and so should be avoided. Presenting immediately after a coffee break provides the opportunity to mingle with delegates, creating a bond with the audience. All delegates will be refreshed, avoiding the influence of fidgets on your presentation. Following these guidelines will provide you, the budding Power Presenter, with a head start when organising your conference presentation slot.

As the delegates take their seats, have you ever stopped to think where they are sitting, because as a Power Presenter this is another aspect whereby you can gain a real advantage over other speakers. The very orientation of the room is the subject of the next chapter and, although the topic may sound insignificant, as you'll soon discover, room orientation can have significant influence on a number of presentation aspects.

What is the orientation of the room?

"Every orientation presupposes a disorientation."
Hans Magnus Enzenberger

The orientation of a room plays an important element in the success of a presentation. If the orientation is right then delegates are more likely to absorb the information coming their way; get the orientation wrong and messages can be lost because of the discomfort felt by the delegates. The configuration and orientation of the room may also be different from the environment that all of your practice took part in. This could lead to increasing any nerves you may be experiencing prior to the presentation.

When considering the orientation of a room the key question to consider is where is the action going to take place? For a PowerPoint presentation then that is fairly easy, as the focus will be on the front screen. For other presentations it may revolve around a piece of equipment or a model structure.

Once the focal point of the presentation is established the next stage is to consider the audience. All audience members should have a clear line of sight to the focal point with no inbuilt distraction caused by the body movement of other audience members. The design and layout of the venue for your presentation will hopefully allow this principle to take place. The orientation of a room can fall into two categories, namely 'static' or 'mobile'.

An example of a static room orientation would be a lecture theatre where seats are mounted in rows as in a university for example. Occasionally, before the banking of seats starts, some theatres may have approximately ten rows of seats on a level surface. If this is the case, check that those in later rows can easily see the bottom of the presentation screen with other audience members sitting in front of them.

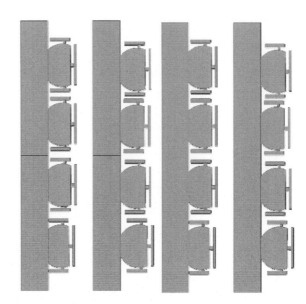

Lecture theatre arrangement.

An example of a mobile room would be where tables and chairs are completely portable; venues such as hotels, smaller conference rooms tend to have this option applied. This type of flexibility leads into a further consideration.

Boardroom arrangement.

When considering a PowerPoint presentation, any viewing angle for an audience member glancing from the side is going to be uncomfortable. This type of viewing angle is generated if a room is configured as a boardroom or as a horseshoe arrangement.

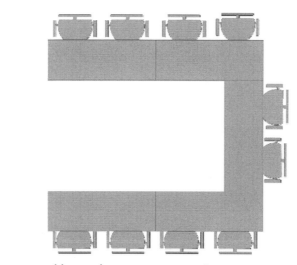

Horseshoe arrangement.

A herringbone configuration offers all audience members a good viewing angle to the presentation; at the same time allowing the presenter to move around the delegates, allowing them to feel engaged in the presentation.

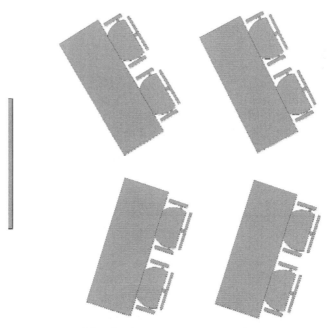

Herringbone arrangement

Depending on the size of the venue, what I class as a wedding orientation may be laid out.

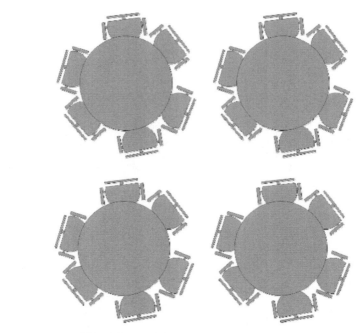

Wedding table arrangement

This consists of a series of round tables containing 6-10 delegates. As a presenter trying to convey an important message this orientation has no positive attraction. It leads to poor viewing angles and encourages audience members to lose attention; if possible avoid at all costs for the presentation to be a success.

A square room arrangement holds similar shortcomings as the wedding table arrangement. Not all delegates have a favourable viewing angle to the focal point of the presentation. This will undoubtedly lead to discomfort for some during the presentation, with the key message being possibly lost. As a presenter you are always on the outer circle of the delegates, whereas with the horseshoe arrangement walking into the delegates is a possibility.

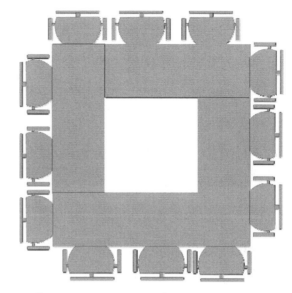

Square arrangement

In a training environment where circulation is important then a different set of criteria needs to be applied. A lecture theatre allows no immediate interaction with delegates; access to the delegate is restricted should a specific question be asked. The horseshoe and herringbone allow free-flowing movement amongst delegates.

If a series of breakout sessions involving group work is required following an initial presentation, then using a separate room in a wedding orientation works extremely well. Delegates can interact with each other and, as a presenter, your movement is unrestricted.

With regard to room orientation one room does not fit all solutions. Consideration needs to be given to the key objective and the best way to convey a message. If you have access to rooms allowing furniture to be moved, then move tables and chairs into an orientation that you as the presenter are comfortable with. Arriving sufficiently early at a venue will allow the time required to assess and then implement your changes.

The room must match your style of presenting and allow the key messages to be conveyed to the audience in a comfortable environment. With the room issue addressed, what about you in relation to the room? Can you, should you and will you move around as you present? In the next chapter, we'll look at how much licence you have as a presenter to move around and the impact this can have on your audience.

Freedom to move

"A static hero is a public liability. Progress grows out of motion."
Richard E. Byrd

So your presentation is designed and rehearsed with regard to slide transitions and narrative. One important element to include is the freedom available at the venue with regard to your movement and interaction with the audience.

During this section, consideration will be given to four main areas of freedom: Lectern, stage, audience and video conference. A final question will be addressed whether one presentation fits all of these staged scenarios.

Let us begin by touching on the subject of lecterns – Reading desks with a slanted top, usually placed on a stand or some other form of support. When attending exhibitions with built-in conference areas within the exhibition stands, more often than not a lectern will be in place to the side of the screen. This is a stage design which may portray a sense of imposed knowledge but as a presentation stance lacks an incredible amount of flexibility. To a nervous presenter the lectern does offer a comfort zone in two key areas. It firstly provides cover for shaking hands and secondly a safety area from the audience. As a Power Presenter you should not be suffering from either of these mental constraints. With a well-rehearsed presentation your presentation will flow, allaying any nerves. When presenting from a lectern, the fixture itself will automatically provide a disconnection from the audience. Search *YouTube* for videos of the late Steve Jobs of Apple Inc. These will show a brilliant presenter who rarely used a lectern.

Another reason conference organisers use lecterns is to have a built-in audio system. With a large venue this is obviously a necessity but wireless microphones are inexpensive and provide the flexibility to move away from the lectern. I would suggest at all times request a wireless microphone rather than the built-in lectern system.

Presenting from a stage does allow the freedom to move and engage the audience without inbuilt barriers such as lecterns. Having the freedom to stand at the side of the screen will allow hand gestures to welcome text and graphics onto the screen. This combination increases the positive mental messages for delegates. Having the freedom to move around a stage does not mean becoming an overexcited whirlwind of energy. Any energy must be channelled correctly into the presentation. To be centre stage with an audience hanging on every word may be intimidating for some presenters and nerves such as shaking hands will be exposed. Further chapters in this book deal with stance and how to calm nerves, allowing a confident Power Presenter to develop.

When questions are asked at the end or during set points in a presentation, being on the stage allows you, the presenter to move to address the questioner in an engaging manner rather than simply talking from behind a lectern. This engagement again builds the mental image that delegates will take away with them.

Smaller auditoriums provide the opportunity to present from within the audience. Having this ability makes the presentation very intimate; a situation where this potential will arise is during corporate meetings. When presenting from within the audience it is essential to work with a presentation clicker to advance slides. This avoids the constant need to walk to your laptop to perform the advance operation. The use of presentation clickers and their merits are covered in greater detail elsewhere. The choice of presenting from within the audience can set a particular tone due to the intimate environment. If news of redundancy needs to be conveyed to work colleagues, or the delivery of a bereavement message, being part of the audience can soften the news.

The general interaction that can be achieved from presenting in this manner is important and should not be underestimated. With the presenter in close proximity to the audience then audience members pay increased attention.

The potential to be performing a presentation through video conference facilities does immediately have a productivity saving with regard to costs in travel, hotels and subsistence. Sharing slides for the presentation over the Internet whilst talking into a camera can take a little getting used to. The limitations in such a process are that of body movement to enhance the message of the slide presentation. Conference facilities tend to be set around a boardroom table configuration which restricts the movement of the presenter. For this reason careful consideration needs to be given to the narrative accompanying each slide in the presentation.

With these four presentation options with regard to movement, is one presentation suitable for each delivery method? The whole essence of a successful presentation is the interaction between the body visual and the visual stimulation from the slide. Presenting from behind a lectern automatically restricts the body involvement so readily available by presenting on the stage. Likewise, the restriction of video conference presentation techniques creates similar issues with body movement and emphasis. Both of these methods of presenting are likely to require the slide itself to include a greater amount of information. A balance needs to be set though in not overpowering the slide with 'noise'. As a presenter it should not mean falling into the safety net of using the slide as a script, these two should still be separated out regardless of the presentation style adopted.

To summarise, if at all possible try to avoid presenting from behind a lectern; this option builds a barrier to the audience and a restriction for transmitting the key messages to delegates. Importantly, each venue may be slightly different with regard to layout and facilities. Under these circumstances give serious consideration for the need to be flexible in the design of the PowerPoint presentation and adapt if required. Including small changes will make the difference for the Power Presenter.

Developing this topic further, the next chapter provides tools you can use to help you literally own the stage. Predominately, the chapter covers moving around the stage and when to do so. It also touches on your focus as a presenter. These aspects combine to help you have a greater stage presence.

Standing, moving and focussing

"I used to say of Napoleon that his presence on the field made the difference of forty thousand men."
Duke of Wellington

Within this next chapter, we'll look at three specific tools you can use to further introduce professionalism into your presentation delivery. Firstly, we'll explore what seems to be a basic aspect of presenting – How to stand. Then we'll add to that by looking at whether you should be still or rove around the stage or even mix it, in with the audience. Finally in this section, we offer advice so that you come across as engaging with the entire audience more than just standing there and staring out into the auditorium or worse, at your notes on the screen next to you.

So to begin with, have you ever stopped to think how you should stand when in front of an audience? Here are some basic dos and don'ts. Firstly, although you want to exude confidence and feel that way internally too, be careful not to resemble an actor in an old silent movie who greatly exaggerates each movement of their body and stance they make so as to 'act' the words they can't use. Try to develop a technique for standing naturally, but with a quiet air of confidence. Hold your head up, relax (as much as possible) and try to imagine you are giving the presentation to your own family in your own sitting room. Next, feel free to move around. It is your stage and as we've already discussed, act like you own it, all of it. Nonchalantly walk around the various parts of it, try to pair up with the screen and present the audience with a professional looking double act. Finally on how to stand, beware distractions in your pockets. One way to look calm and in control is to have a hand in your pocket as you present. A sure-fire way to spoil this impression is if you then play with things in the said pocket, such as jangling change etc.

We've already mentioned owning the stage, but the point we'd like to reiterate here is how too many presenters are metaphorically glued behind the lectern, and petrified to come out from behind it. It may be that they need the mental security of knowing they can refer to their notes at a moment's notice. But if you have followed the advice on rehearsal, then you'll know that you don't need the notes and so are free to visually add to the messages you are communicating with the use of your body. Another point here is that all too often (and frankly, we've no idea why) the lectern is on the wrong side of the stage. It should be on the left as the audience sees it so that the presenter feeds information across the screen in a left to right manner. The same way people in the western world read, as is discussed elsewhere in this book.

Some presenters and TV celebrities have a very nice trick of engaging with particular members of their audience. At the beginning of their show, they talk to a small number of audience members individually and often elicit their names; then, as the show progresses, they'll continue to refer back to these individuals by name. This is yet another way by which you as a presenter can appear at the top of your Power Presenting game. This may however appear somewhat daunting; having to remember the names of strangers what with all the other stuff you might have going round your head while on stage. So here's an easier solution. Just pick three areas of the audience (say, left, middle and right, rows 3 to 6) and regularly visually look in these directions as you present. To the audience, you will appear to be engaging with the entire room and so come across as more engaging.

Some people will try to mix with the audience before the presentation begins (often a good idea) and so will have developed a connection with certain members and they can then refer to them during their show, providing they can see them in the audience. To be honest, they don't always need to see them. If they know who they are and can recall what they talked about before the presentation, they can just namedrop to demonstrate to the rest of the audience how professional they are.

So in summary with regard to what can be collectively termed stage presence, there are a number of aspects you should consider as a Power Presenter. Firstly, what do you look like physiologically? Remember, our inner mental state often reflects our physiological poise, so you need to physically present yourself as you want to feel. Secondly here, don't be rooted to the spot; you will appear much more engaging to the audience if you move around the stage – Own it and use it accordingly. By moving around, you are giving yourself the opportunity of appearing to engage more with those watching you and also, you can use the movement to great effect to add emphasis to points you are making as you present.

When it comes to presenting PowerPoint to audiences, all too often almost all of the focus goes on the slide design and the message contained within it. What we're sharing here is that the way in which the message is delivered is equally important if you want the audience to fully engage with it. We'd go as far as to say that if all the effort goes into the slide design and messages, and no consideration is given to the way in which the content is presented, specifically the physiology of the presenter, then why not send the presentation out by email and not bother getting all of the audience in the same room? A presentation, by its very name needs to be presented. So as a Power Presenter, you need to understand all you can about presenting and one of the best assets you have up there on stage is your own body and how you use it.

In this chapter, we touched on where you should look with regard to engaging the audience. In the next one, we'll again focus on your area of visual attention, but this time, more in relation to the messages you are delivering.

Where to look

"A man should look for what is, and not for what he thinks should be."
Albert Einstein

It has been quantified that around 70% of human communication is visual. Whatever you look at you mentally process and your audience does the same. In this next section we'll look at, well, where to look. As a presenter you have considerable control over your audience and you can choreograph many of the actions they will take during your presentation.

To demonstrate just how much you can manage the direct visual attention of others, try this next time you are in a shopping street. Stand still and look up, what do most passers by do? They look up. This is how loyally humans will follow another person's sightline. It's also worth noting that humans prefer to look down as opposed to up. This is another throwback to our evolution, caused by the fact that originally we walked on all fours all those thousands of years ago. So when we stood erect, the natural balancing mechanisms in our heads were out of sync and so as a workaround, tilting our heads 30 degrees forwards resynchronises our internal balance mechanism.

So how does this knowledge help the presenter on stage? Firstly and fundamentally, most screens are positioned so that all of the audience can see them. Therefore they tend to be above their natural eye lines; ergo, the audience has to look up to view the presentation. If you want something to be looked at more than something else, one tool you can use is to locate it lower down the screen. This is contrary to how many presentation designers design their slides, which are typically headline at the top and then work downwards. Although this isn't wrong, having a key message at the bottom of the screen will be in the natural sight lines of the audience more and can be effectively used for emphasis and visual reinforcement of the key headline.

As a Power Presenter, we can control when we want to make the audience really visually concentrate on a key message or component on a slide. All we have to do is visibly direct our gaze towards the visual aspect we want the audience to look at and viola, they'll do just that (remember the standing in the street looking up example?). You can very effectively manage the attention of your audience by managing precisely when you turn and look at the main screen they too are facing. Naturally, you can do the opposite if there is something on screen that you don't want them to pay too much attention too.

While we're on the subject of where the presenter should look as they present, apart from the choreographed glances at the main screen, there are some best practice techniques you can adopt. To begin with, don't fixate on any notes, script or laptop screen in front of you – Look up and out at the audience. This way, you'll visually engage with them and appear to be communicating directly with them. To take this a stage further, pick out three items, locations or people in the room that are spaced evenly, left, centre and right (mid to rear of the audience). Now, as you present, regularly look in each predetermined direction. This will have the result of the entire audience feeling that you are talking to them.

You can now engage with more of the audience as you present and you can manage when you want them to really pay (visual) attention to the content on screen.

Politicians employ a subtle tactic to endear their audience to themselves and to make out that they are more popular than often is the case. Watch as they walk towards a speaking lectern, how they appear to be waving and acknowledging specific individuals they appear to know, and often also mouthing words to them. This gives viewers the perception that they have friends in the audience and that they are well liked. Some professional presenters employ the same ruse to make the audience believe that the presenter is well known and liked by some peers in the room.

There is another point to make while we're on the subject of where we should look as we are presenting and that is, you should be mindful of distractions to your flow. For example, at a recent conference, a real live lion cub was brought into the back of the hall as part of a charity fund raiser for the protection of lions in Africa. This had a couple of profound impacts: Firstly, the presenter completely lost the flow of what they were supposed to be talking about; and secondly, more and more of the audience turned to face the lion. When something unexpected happens, be prepared and ready to take action. In the case of the lion, it would have been better to introduce a break and then return to the presentation afterwards.

As a final recommendation relating to where to look, try to pay attention to the audience, and in particular how engaged they appear to be. For example, what percentage is looking at you? Have some disengaged and are maybe doodling, playing with their mobile phones or, worse still, attending to emails on iPads and laptops? Over time you'll develop a form of sixth sense here and you'll be able to read an audience quickly and accurately. Once you are able to get a sense of their mindsets, you can take action to manage it. For example, you can skip to the next section, introduce a break or hopefully, if they are all still fully engaged, just carry on as you are.

In summary, there are a number of considerations with regard to where you, the presenter should look while you present. Don't simply read a script; engage with different areas of the audience and manage when you want their visual attention on the screen by using your own direction of gaze to lead theirs. Finally, as you are looking out at the audience, frequently inspect how engaged they appear to be with your presentation and be prepared to act on the instant visual feedback you receive.

In fact, you as the centre of attention during your presentation, have considerable influence over where the audience look and although you can choreograph and manage this as discussed in the last chapter, the audience will automatically respond in certain ways to wherever you are on stage. Therefore, the next chapter details why you should stand on the left of the screen for a lot of the time you are revealing content.

Stand on the left – Where humans look

"Language commonly stresses only one side of any interaction."
Gregory Bateson

Here's a very specific aspect of effective presenting. Where should you, the presenter, stand? The same topic is covered in other ways in terms of whether to walk amongst the audience, and how to deal with the limiting aspect of any lectern or other objects that it is possible to hide behind.

Specifically here, we'll look at how the presenter and the presentation screen, complete with its content, can combine to optimum effect.

To begin with, think about five presentations you recall and list down where the presenter was stood in relation to the screen; to the left (as you look at them), the right, in front of it (we hope not), below it, etc.

Next, we'd like you to conduct the same exercise, but this time provide details relating to five poor presentations you recall.

What we want to do now is arm you with another tool to make sure presentations you give in future are recalled as being good by others and, equally importantly, that the content of which is more embedded in their memories afterwards.

The fact is that, in the western world, people read from left to right and the same is true when they look at a PowerPoint screen. So as a Power Presenter, if you stand on the left of the screen (as the audience sees you) you are then able to make comments and feed in the screen content in a way most naturally for the audience to mentally absorb. To see this in action, watch the majority of weather forecasts on TV – Where does the presenter stand? – And note how they feed in the chart content to align with what they are saying at that moment.

Learn to stand with the screen on your left so that when you look towards it, the audience will follow and they will be doing so from left to right on the screen and so most ably to mentally absorb the messages. Even if the venue is set up so that you are almost forced to stand in the wrong place (you'd be amazed how many lecterns are placed on the right of the stage as we've already said from the audience's perspective), explore ways of getting yourself in a location on stage that results in the screen being on your left, particularly when delivering your key messages.

In summary, stand in front of the audience with the screen to *your* left. When delivering key messages, link your words, behaviour and the screen in a seamless left to right action. Finally, don't let the design of the venue govern where you present from – Use the science of how humans read.

Going back to the positives of your presentation performance, let's turn our attention to how much attention you want to attract and in fact whether on occasions you may want to divert attention away from something (such as bad news).

Creating attention and distraction

"A good advertisement is one which sells the product without drawing attention to itself."
David Ogilvy

When we're designing and delivering our presentations, we all strive (consciously or sub-consciously) to draw attention to different aspects of what we are saying and visualising on screen. In this next section, we'll look at a number of techniques designed specifically to draw the attention of the audience to different aspects of our presentation. We'll also offer advice regarding instances when you may want to do just the opposite: That is to say, divert the attention of the audience away from your message (such as when delivering bad news).

But to begin with, let's have a quick résumé of what attention actually is. In 1890, William James, in his textbook *Principles of Psychology*, remarked: *"Everyone knows what attention is. It is the taking possession by the mind, in clear and vivid form, of one out of what seem several simultaneously possible objects or trains of thought. Focalization, concentration, of consciousness are of its essence. It implies withdrawal from some things in order to deal effectively with others, and is a condition which has a real opposite in the confused, dazed, scatterbrained state which in French is called distraction."*

It is widely acknowledged that the human brain is only able to be cognitively attentive towards a fraction of what is going on around it. Although estimates vary, 5% is a good benchmark to use. That being so, it follows that an audience can only pay attention to a part of the presentation they are attending. For that very reason, the Power Presenter needs to factor into their presentation design which are the key messages that they do and don't want the audience to pay attention to. For example, a senior executive may want to promote the fact that sales are up, but be less overt about the fact that profit margins are down.

With that in mind, here are a few tips and tricks to direct the mind of your audience as you present. Firstly, as you turn and look at the screen to your side, so too will most of the audience. You can further strengthen their attention by using hand movements at the same time to pinpoint their focus on a particular aspect on screen. We can also use position on screen to help draw attention to specifics. We in the western world typically read from left to right; therefore, we'll scan the screen starting on the left. That's where you can initially grab their attention.

Here's an interesting technique and it involves how the human brain processes letters and words. Scientists some decades ago identified that words were read more quickly if they were in a combination of upper and lower case letters (as opposed to being in all CAPITALS). This is evidenced if you look at the majority of road signs in use today. In New York, the powers that be agreed with the science and spent an alleged 25 million dollars changing signs to upper and lower case. So if you want something to stand out and it's one of only a few words on the screen, avoid all capitals. Good for shouting in emails, but not so effective for Power Presenting.

Next, recognise the value of contrast. If we said that a single orange triangle on screen stands out, it would be true. But if there are lots of triangles on screen then the effect would be nullified. In that instance, it would be better to put a single circle on the screen of triangles for maximum stand out.

If there is a lot of one colour on screen, use an opposite one to stand out. Incidentally, if you'd like to know more about colours and their opposites, simply type 'colour wheel' into your preferred Internet search engine. A colour wheel (also referred to as a colour circle) is a visual representation of colours arranged according to their chromatic relationship.

As a final method of drawing attention towards a specific point, force your audience to layer their thinking towards the point being made in terms of having to use some or all of their senses. For example, the presenter may ask the audience to visualise something and at the same time hear an associated sound, smell something related or even touch and taste. This builds in the audience's heads and fully occupies their conscious attention (and requires assistance from the sub-conscious too).

We also promised to explore how to divert the attention of an audience away from something and here are a few pointers. Firstly, do the opposite of anything aimed at increasing attention. Secondly, use incongruity to prevent the message from being properly processed in the audience's minds. An example of this would be to have your uttered words, bodily movements and on screen content all contradictory from a scale perspective. One thousand redundancies mentioned, while hand gestures indicate tiny in some way and the screen content either reinforces small and insignificant or actively offers another message to be processed, such as record bonuses to key staff.

Relatively recently, politicians and their spin doctors have recognised how to manage bad news. For example, on the day of the tragic 9/11 World Trade Center massacre a UK spin doctor was actually caught after sending an email as New York's twin towers burned, suggesting that 11th September was a good day to 'bury' bad news. This action led to her and the then transport department press chief quitting their jobs. You can use aspects of your presentation to very much the same effect by using a fantastic eye-catching slide that distracts the audience away from a particular message that you have to convey to them. Alternatively, the physical size on screen can alter the perception of how important something is; a 12% increase in massive letters next to 25% fall in much smaller letters will distort the importance toward the 12% message.

A final way to distract attention is to actually turn the audience to focus on itself by using a psychological tool known as projection. This entails explaining what parts of the audience are probably thinking (in other words, what you want them to think of) and then saying things like 'at least half of the people I spoke to earlier, now in this auditorium expressed (then insert the opinion you want to convey)'.

In summary, there are many ways you can attract attention to key messages and divert the audience away from specific points. The key is to recognise the fact that you can and indeed need to manage the attention of those you are presenting to. That way, more of them will leave the event thinking precisely what you want them to think.

Now let's look at using our senses to add emphasis to what we are communicating: The next chapter looks at how we can optimise the memorising abilities of our audiences.

Dual encoding – Multi sensory processing

"All credibility, all good conscience, all evidence of truth come only from the senses."

Friedrich Nietzsche

In this section, we'll look at how, as Power Presenters, we can more efficiently communicate what we want to say to those in the audience. Efficiency here relates to how well we get the audience to remember the key aspects of what we tell them. In fact, almost any presentation can be said to be only as effective as how much of its content gets hard-wired into the memories of the audience. And that leads on to the fact that each member of the audience has two different forms of memory; long term memory and short term working memory (both covered in more detail earlier in this book). Any memory strategies that involve simultaneous visual and verbal processing (such as watching a PowerPoint presentation while listening to the presenter) have to involve the short term working memory, as coordination of different sensory inputs is one of its key roles. Strategies designed to actively cause simultaneous multi-sensory processing are known as 'dual encoding' strategies.

Presentation techniques that involve concurrent verbal and visual encoding (dual encoding) have been shown to be significantly more powerful than singular verbal or visual encoding. The use of dual encoding helps information pass through into long term memory by creating firstly, a more multi-sensory related and therefore emotional piece of information, and secondly, because the learner creates multiple retrieval routes to the same information. The long term benefits of dual encoding were recognised by Paivio and Csapo (1960) who identified that concepts presented once in visual form and simultaneously once in verbal form were remembered better than when the same concepts were presented twice in visual form or twice in verbal form.

The very nature of a PowerPoint presentation is in itself a dual encoding strategy. The presenter speaks, so providing the verbal component while the images on screen represent the visual aspect. An important point to make here is that if the person is speaking and the same words appear on the screen then this isn't dual encoding, because the spoken and written word would be processed in part in the same areas of the brain and so nullifying any dual encoding benefit. However, if the presenter is verbally referring to something specific such as an increase in annual profits, while at the same time there is a line chart showing (even exaggerating) the visual concept of increasing or growing, this involves the audience members having to dual encode the point. Incidentally, techniques for exaggerating this point include making the line in the line chart more than 10 points wide and having an arrow (pointing upwards) on the end. Also, the scale on the vertical axis should be adjusted so that the growth, however small, goes from the bottom of the scale to the top. In other words, don't show an increase from 10% to 20% on a chart with a scale of 0% to 100%. Instead, adjust the vertical axis scale to have a minimum of 10% and a maximum of 20%, in this example.

A simple way to understand how to design an effective dual encoding strategy would be to design the words spoken to work without the need for anything on screen and the on-screen presentation to be a visual representation of the same story or message set. Imagine the screen is the set of a silent movie (without sub-titles). The result of this approach is that when you bring the words and visuals together, the whole is greater than the sum of the parts. The resultant presentation is more likely to be an effective communication designed on solid dual encoding strategy.

The excellent technique of dual encoding is a great way for us as Power Presenters to get our messages away more effectively. There is also another benefit of this psychological technique. For the Power Presenter, combining verbal rehearsal and visualisation can also be a benefit during presentation rehearsal (as again this is an example of dual encoding). So, as a rehearsal strategy, try to verbalise your presentation while at the same time visualising what would be on the screen. This way, you will be more efficiently storing your presentation in your long term memory ready for the big day. To really optimise your own dual encoding rehearsal, speak your words emotionally and overlay your mental visualisation with emotion. That is the way to get more information into your long term memory and so to learn more efficiently.

In summary, dual encoding can help us as Power Presenters in a number of ways. Firstly, simultaneously presenting verbal and visual content is proven to be a more effective means of embedding key messages into the brains of the audience. Secondly, using the same theory as we rehearse our presentations can improve our learning efficiency. As a final point on this subject, as you become more accustomed to incorporating dual encoding into your presentation design, you'll find that you are unable to use bullet points on the screen to any beneficial effect; good!

The next chapter expands on the powerful technique of dual encoding and provides insights relating to how you can further optimise its effect by introducing aspects of synchronisation.

Synchronised dual encoding

"Always aim at complete harmony of thought and word and deed. Always aim at purifying your thoughts and everything will be well."
Mahatma Gandhi

In the last chapter, we explored the subject of dual encoding and demonstrated how it can dramatically improve the learning efficiency of your audience in relation to what you are presenting to them. In this next section, we'll look at how you can further refine your presenting style to make sure that even more of your presentation becomes firmly embedded within the brains of your audience.

Having established that by *forcing* the audience to simultaneously process verbal messages and visual imagery disproportionately improves their learning ability, we now want to discuss adding synchronisation to your sensory output. To illustrate this technique in action, let's use the example of the increased profits line graph mentioned earlier. At a basic dual encoding level, you talk of increased profits while visually showing an exaggerated visual form of increase and growth (in this case the line chart). To introduce synchronisation to this dual encoding example, you would introduce an animation of the line of the line chart so that it appeared from left (0%) to right (10%) across the screen on the click of the mouse (or presentation clicker). Now you have all the components of synchronised dual encoding and you just need to effectively execute them. To do that in this example, just before you mentioned 'increased profits' (the actual words), your eyes would turn to the screen. This causes the audience to direct their attention more towards the visual aspects (i.e. the screen). Then you would raise your arm to the start point of the line in the line chart, say the words 'increased profits' and as you utter 'increased' click your presentation clicker (or mouse) so that the ascending line appears to grow right in front of the eyes of the audience as they are fixated on the screen and as they hear the word 'profit'.

Effective synchronised dual encoding consists of four different components that are then executed in an almost choreographed manner. Firstly, you need the correct verbal message. This should be a specific spoken point, no longer than a few words in length (ideally less than nine words). Secondly, you need the supporting on-screen imagery; something that visually reinforces the point you are making (no clip art, please). The third component of your synchronisation is a form of animation; this may be as simple as appearing on screen or a more technically advanced animation. The fourth and final component is the execution and timing. In other words, how components 1 to 3 work with each other. The result is a clear message delivered powerfully and professionally.

Make sure that when you are gesturing towards the screen as content is to appear that the content appears in a method congruent with the hand movement. For example, if you look to the screen and make a point, at a time when you are stood at the left of the screen (as the audience sees it) and you gesture towards the left edge of the screen, the content should, if entering, do so in a way that appears as if it is coming from your gesturing hand. In other words, it could be said that you use your gestures to pull, push, inflate, and rub out, etc. specific things that enter and or leave the screen. You can have quite a lot of fun with this technique and will no doubt develop your own style over time. A personal favourite of mine is to click my fingers as if I'm directing the screen content to do as I say.

If you want to learn from others using synchronised dual encoding, look no further than the trusted weathermen and women on the TV. As they talk of a cold front moving in from the east, their hand gestures in front of the map behind them from east to west and at the same time, the familiar isobars (lines) are animated to move in the same direction.

News reporters are also good exponents of synchronised dual encoding and in recent years, as the screens behind them have got ever larger, they now have to physically walk around the studio to carry out their presentation (remember owning the stage?).

Here's an application of synchronised dual encoding that you may find beneficial if you find yourself in more confrontational situations on stage. For example, imagine you are in a political debate with a member of an opposing party stood next to you and the pair of you are in front of an audience. In this instance, every time you utter a negative word direct the audience's visual attention towards your opponent (by using either your direction of gaze and/or subtle hand or arm movement). Conversely, every time you use a positive word or phrase, gesture towards yourself. This will have the effect of the audience associating more negativity with your opponent and more positivity with you.

Back to the main subject of adding synchronicity to your dual encoding, the key to its overall effectiveness is the timing. So it is important that as you develop this technique, you create your own methods of knowing what to say, when to click for an animation and precisely when and where to direct your gaze. This is actually much easier than it may appear. What you are actually doing is creating a number of single-scripted behaviours, each of which is activated, once learned and rehearsed, by a single trigger. One way to learn your own synchronisation is to imagine that as you state your key point, your body actually carries it out (pulls a line across the screen, for example).

Once again, the subject of synchronised dual encoding provides evidence that Power Presenting is much more than just reading bullet points off a screen. It is in fact a combination of communications media, including the different senses of the presenter, with on-screen imagery and activity, all brought together so as to engage and enthral the audience. Next time you are asked to give a presentation, bear in mind the breadth of the communication opportunity that gives you.

You should also bear in mind what is meant by communication (and even the word presentation). As the next chapter explains, what we say can account for only a fraction of what we communicate to an audience.

Words are only 7% of the meaning

"Words mean more than what is set down on paper. It takes the human voice to infuse them with deeper meaning."
Maya Angelou

In this next chapter we'll look at what is, in our opinion, one of the most under-recognised golden nuggets any Power Presenter could ever wish to know. This is a discovery made by Professor Albert Mehrabian when he was pioneering the understanding of communications back in the 1960s. Aside from his many and various other fascinating works, Mehrabian's research provided the basis for the widely quoted and often much over-simplified statistic for the effectiveness of spoken communications. The following is the common and over-simplified interpretation of Mehrabian's findings, which is quoted and applied by many people to cover all communications – often without reference to Mehrabian, although Mehrabian's work is the derivation:

- 7% of meaning is in the words that are spoken.

- 38% of meaning is paralinguistic (the way that the words are said).

- 55% of meaning is in facial expression.

It is understandable that many people prefer short concise statements. However, if you recognise the simplified form of the Mehrabian formula you must also understand the true context of Mehrabian's findings. As a minimum you must accept that the formula applies to communications of feelings and attitudes (emotions).

Here is a more precise (and necessarily detailed) representation of Mehrabian's findings than is typically cited or applied:

- 7% of message pertaining to feelings and attitudes is in the words that are spoken.

- 38% of message pertaining to feelings and attitudes is paralinguistic (the way that the words are said).

- 55% of message pertaining to feelings and attitudes is in facial expression.

Albert Mehrabian's famous statistics about words, tone of voice and non-verbal communication offer valuable insights and opportunities to presenters regarding how they can enhance what they say, with the way they say it (ergo, present it) and how the screen content can greatly improve how well the message gets across to the audience.

So now, let's look at the fact that as a Power Presenter you have more than just two tools to present with – the words you say and what is on the screen (hopefully not the same words again). In fact, you have four tools at your disposal; the extra ones being the tone of voice you use when presenting and your entire body language with which you communicate while presenting. Ok, so you can have a great presentation, expertly designed, well rehearsed and full of captivating content and key messages, but if you want to really engage the audience to the full, then the best way to do so is by doing so emotionally. Emotions are mentally processed much more quickly than cognitive thought and are more powerful too.

As you are crafting your Power Presentations, start to do so by using all four communications tools at your disposal. Get your script (or patter as it is known) right and make sure the screen content works in harmony with what you are saying. But go the extra yard and you'll really reap the benefits as a presenter. Pay particular attention to the tone of voice you use while speaking publicly. As an exercise, when you are rehearsing, record yourself and then play it back (if an audio only recording, do so while viewing and building the relevant screen content). Is there enough emotion in your voice? Is it the right emotion at the right time? Or perhaps it is just fear, right? Well from now on we're going to practise our tone of voice, particularly in relation to when we're delivering our key messages. If we want to be positive, then talk in an upbeat tone. When delivering more sombre information, then sound sincere at least.

And remember that the most powerful communication tool we have at our disposal is our body (including our face). Get hold of a camcorder, and as you practise delivering your presentation, design and refine what you communicate non-verbally to your audience. This may be as simple as making sure that you don't make body language errors such as covering your mouth (often received by an audience as lying, remember?).

With these new-found communications tools, you can start to emotionally engage with the audience at a much more sophisticated and powerful level. Now you can say something, use your tone of voice for emphasis, allow the screen content to assist in embedding your message into the brains of the audience and your body can hit the message home.

In our own research, we have quantified that by using a four-pronged communication strategy like the one we've just described, audience recall of the content of a presentation has risen from around 20% a week after the event, to more than 70%.

Finally, don't worry if at the beginning, you don't feel blessed with the multi-faceted communications expertise of a top Hollywood actor or actress. Because as you start to record and study your own rehearsals, you'll very quickly realise just how little effort it takes to transcend from a run of the mill presenter, to something a whole lot more advanced and effective.

In summary, you have the words you utter as a core communications tool. However, they are just the tip of the iceberg in terms of what you are communicating with the audience and how effectively you can impart information to them. As you develop as a Power Presenter, use the screen content to add emphasis and 'colour' to what you are saying. Then bring your tone of voice to the fore and recognise how much more effectively you can underscore your key messages. Finally, don't forget that thing that is responsible for 55% of the feelings and attitude you are communicating – your body. Pay particular attention to your body language to make sure your physiology is congruent with your message. In addition, look at your own facial expressions, with a view to being able to use them as another level of communication support for your presentation message.

There has been so much written about what was originally Albert Mehrabian's 7%, 38%, 55% rule, that it isn't possible to fully cover it here. Albert Mehrabian's famous statistics about words, tone of voice and non-verbal communication offer a valuable plethora of opportunities to us as presenters regarding how we can enhance what we say, with the way we say it (ergo, present it) and how the screen content can greatly improve how well the message gets across to your audience. We strongly recommend that you dig a little more deeply into this subject and as a starting point, Albert Mehrabian's key book is *Silent Messages*, which contains lots of information about non-verbal communications (body language).

With all this movement being talked about, we should explain about how you can break the chain between you and the laptop, lectern or fixed presentation controlling device. In the next chapter, we'll explain just how a small and inexpensive electronic device can literally transform your freedom on stage and your presence and stage ownership.

Remote presentation but not a laser

"All the best stories in the world are but one story in reality – the story of escape. It is the only thing which interests us all and at all times, how to escape."
Walter Bagehot

If you want to deliver a truly memorable, engaging and professional presentation, not only do you need the right presentation but you also need the right tools of the trade. One of these tools is a wireless presentation remote clicker – a small handheld device that gives you direct control of presentation navigation.

The main advantage of using one of these gadgets is that they allow the presenter to move away from the lectern or laptop and yet still advance their presentation. In actual fact, very often the main difference between a good presenter and a poor one is that the former appears to be more connected to the content they are presenting on the screen and one way to do this is to get closer to it and to move in and around it more intimately. To achieve this you need to break the umbilical cord type link between yourself and the lectern and any controls bolted to it.

Once you accept that one of these little gadgets is a great help to you as a Power Presenter, let's explore them in a bit more detail. If you type 'Remote Presenter' into *Google*, you will be offered almost 12,000,000 pages about them. That's an awful lot of information about something that few people use but that costs less than £50. Having used a number of different remote presenters over time, we think that one of the best ones is the basic unit by Kensington (Si 600). This USB-controlled device offers just four buttons: Advance to next click/slide, rewind to previous one and black screen (useful during any question and answer or debating sessions). Some of you may note that we've only talked of three buttons and that is because the fourth one should only ever be used in exceptional circumstances – the laser pointer. This may let you highlight a specific small aspect on screen, but just you try and have a steady hand when you do so, and the pointer exaggerates any movement manifold.

There are also a plethora of quite complicated remote presenters available and some offer extra functions, including short cut buttons and other controls. In our experience, this is more of a distraction and should be avoided for all but the most advanced Power Presenters. The main issue is that the more buttons on the remote presenter, then the more chance of pressing the wrong one. As a direct consequence, the people using them have to pay more attention to which button to present and less to delivering their actual presentation. If on the limited number of occasions you need to do more than what is available from a basic remote presenter, then really all you have to do is walk back to the laptop and press one of those big clearly labelled buttons on it.

Incidentally, you may find yourself presenting at a professionally organised event where typically two things happen. Firstly, you are given a small, discreet microphone to wear, consisting of a little backpack transmitter and a small mike to clip to your collar. Remember this, just before and after you present, the mike may well be on and so saying, 'thank f**k that's over' to your colleague as you sit back down may not be the ideal. More relevantly here is that more major event organisers often give you one of their own remote presenters, which in actual fact only trigger an operative to manually advance your presentation. If this is the case try to speak to the operative to devise a means of dealing with accidental double clicks or his/her incorrect navigation.

So in summary, a wireless remote presenter lets you remain in control of your presentation. Conveniently portable and easy-to-use, they free you from the single location of the lectern or directly controlling your laptop and relieve you of distraction. These great little devices allow you to focus on what matters most – your Power Presentation.

Let's now break from all the things surrounding your performance and add in an aspect, often overlooked, sometimes feared and generally underutilised. In the next chapter, we'll talk about... well nothing. The topic is silence and how and when to use it to great effect as part of a presentation.

Pre-slide pausing

"Choose silence of all virtues, for by it you hear other men's imperfections, and conceal your own."
George Bernard Shaw

In this next brief section, we'll take a look at another presenting secret that is used too infrequently. What we're talking about here is using silence, specifically between slides within a presentation.

For some reason, most presenters think that they have to talk continually during their presentations. They seem to be under the impression that any pause must be avoided at all cost. Surprisingly, for some, pausing is a great way to help both the presenter and the audience. By stopping for just a few seconds, you allow all in the room to metaphorically catch their breath and more effectively embed messages.

The pre-slide pause can be used before leaving a completed slide or at the point when the beginnings of a new slide appear on the screen. If you pause at the end of the slide, you give the audience time to finally jointly process the visual content in connection with what you said. This also gives you time to collect yourself and prepare to unfold the story on the next slide.

A more frequently used pause occurs as soon as the title of a new slide appears on the screen. Pausing here lets you the presenter, mentally prepare to tell the tale of that slide. It also gives the audience time to adjust their mindset in readiness for the new topic they're about to be presented.

Because so many presenters are so afraid of pausing, many mistakes are made when they are unsure as to what is coming next. The result is that they try to guess what is on the next slide, verbalise a link, and then on screen appears the beginnings of a totally different slide. The creative use of a pause between slides gives those all-important few seconds to check what is coming next (using whatever prompts are available). This way, the few seconds silence actually makes for a more seamless transition from one slide to another.

Another time to insert a pause into your patter is when something appears on screen that literally takes a bit of mental processing. Here you can either pause as soon as it appears or offer a brief introductory explanation and then pause while the audience mentally makes sense of what they are looking at.

On some occasions, you may want to pause, but not make the break an obvious pause. For example, if you want the audience to take a few seconds to mentally digest a specific point, but don't wish to draw too much attention to the fact. In such situations, calmly ask to be excused so you can take a sip of water. Then as you do so, the audience is left with nothing else to do but to focus on the message.

In the examples of pauses we've mentioned (there are others too), the key is that the pauses help – they help the presenter, the audience or both. So the message is that, as a Power Presenter, you don't have to fill every moment of silence with patter, so don't! Once again, what we're doing is combining the presentation and the presenter in a way that makes the communication of the content as effective as is possible, and in this respect, silence can be a great help that should be encouraged, not feared at all.

In the next chapter, we're going to unashamedly tell you how to cheat when it comes to learning how to improve your presentation performances. In essence we'll encourage you to look to those who are past masters at their professions and then to simply plagiarise the effecting aspects.

Learn from the weathermen and politicians

"Everything that happens, happens as it should, and if you observe carefully, you will find this to be so."
Marcus Aurelius

We'd like to start this section by asking a question. With an estimated 30 million PowerPoint presentations being created every day and so much information available about delivering a presentation to an audience, why is there so little data available that links the two? That is to say, how to use the delivery style and screen content together for optimal effect. In actual fact, that is the aim of this book overall. But we recognise that the business culture of today tends to be impatient for success and in a hurry to earn rapid rewards. Combine with this the host of pressures that force companies to run ever faster just to stand still, and the result is that the focus has shifted from long term health to short term survival (so says Martin Haywood in *Customers Are for Life, Not Just Your Next Bonus*).

What this means at a fundamental level is that many professionals simply don't have the time with which to learn how to create and deliver the most effective of presentations. So for those of you that are in this situation, we'd like to offer some advice regarding how you can improve your presenting without the need to invest too much of your precious time. Incidentally, it is always somewhat amusing that so many people are constantly moaning about having no time, but they always seem to manage to find the several minutes it takes to order and wait for their skinny latte in the local Starbucks or Costa coffee houses (more on these establishments later).

So, for those of you too time starved to use this book to full effect, here are a couple of shortcuts to knowledge that you will be able to utilise. Firstly, watch professional presenters at work: presenters of TV documentaries, weather girls and boys, newscasters and the like. As you watch them, pay particular attention to how they use their bodies (gestures) and the supporting visual content, along with their words, to provide a powerful piece of communication. Recognise the techniques that they have spent months and years honing to perfection that you can go right ahead and copy, plagiarise, steal or 'borrow'. Many of the techniques these professionals use are explained in more detail throughout this book. They are detailed along with explanations as to why they are effective communication tools to use. But for those of you that just need to present more effectively, then leave hunting for supporting evidence as to what works until later.

It isn't only TV presenters that you can learn presenting skills from. A lot of the world's greatest presentations are captured and then made available on *YouTube* and we recommend that you investigate. In addition to *YouTube* and the Internet, you can also begin to pay more objective attention to those delivering presentations that you attend. If nothing else, this will relieve the boredom of sitting through 120 slides of bullet points delivered in a monotone way by somebody with all the presence and charisma of a comatose slug.

In summary, if you simply haven't got the time to invest in learning in a structured way how to improve the presentations you create and the effectiveness with which you deliver them, start by copying those who you regard as masters of the craft. Notice how we recommend that you start by copying others, because the benefits of learning to be more effective and investing time doing so are more than worth the investment. Using the techniques in these pages have helped leading organisations close more deals, improve internal and external training and overall communicate significantly more effectively. As a final point, have you ever noticed how long so many people take to craft and design their presentations and then how little time they spend checking how they will deliver them? Just a brief amount of added time learning from the professionals has so often proved to be such a simple but worthwhile investment; we strongly recommend you make it as your next step. The first step you've already taken by getting hold of this book and beginning to read it.

Now we're going to move on to what is undeniably one of the most important chapters in the book. It discusses one of the key practices of good presenters that is often omitted by less proficient individuals. We're talking about the importance of rehearsing and knowing your presentation inside out, upside down and backwards.

Rehearse, rehearse, and rehearse

"In theory there is no difference between theory and practice. In practice there is."
Yogi Berra

If there is one single thing that will help you have the confidence to deliver the best presentation you can it's having the confidence in your own ability to do so. When we analyse what it is that shakes the confidence of those about to present, then a lot comes down to them simply being in fear of forgetting what to say and going blank. Throughout this book there are a number of tools that can be used to minimise this risk, but in this section we're going to look at how and why you should invest time and effort rehearsing your presentation.

Firstly and as we've already said, the more you know your presentation, the greater your confidence will be when it comes to delivering it. Secondly, the better prepared you are in terms of knowing your content matter, the less of your brain you have to employ to recall it and so the more mental effort you can assign to the delivery of said information.

Having hopefully agreed on the importance of practice and rehearsal, let's look at the different techniques you can use to embed things into your long term memory. Firstly, you should do more than just repeat over and over again what you want to say; you need to get some emotion involved. Emotions are how the human brain best catalogues and later recalls things from memory (much faster and more effectively than cognitive thought). So as you practise your presentation, make it as realistic and multi-sensory as possible. If you will be standing when you present, stand when you rehearse. Develop a mental image of the audience in front of you – Hear any ambient sounds and even take a breath and absorb the smell of the venue. Go even a stage further and try to picture individual members of the audience and direct part of your rehearsal to them. The key here is to practise while your brain is in what is known as an 'associated state'. By this we mean your brain thinks it's at the event, not in the safety of your office or even bedroom. That then is how you add some emotion to your rehearsals and don't be afraid to feel the adulation as you complete it and the audience are truly appreciative.

Now here's a nifty means by which you can remember sequences (alluded to earlier). It may be slides, data or individual aspects of slides (but, please, not bullet points). Start by thinking of a journey you are very familiar with – it may be a trip to work, a walk round your house or even a round at your local golf course. The key is to select a journey you know very well. Next, take each of the items you want to remember and locate them at different locations along your well known journey. Don't just mentally place them there, but do something with each image to make it distinctive. For example, if you decide to mentally place a date as the first thing to recall on your trip round your local golf course, imagine your friend branding the pristine first green with that precise date and then picture it smouldering in front of you. This all helps the brain effectively consign that date to memory in a way that is retrievable.

Another aspect of rehearsal to consider is how to memorise the presentation. Many people just go through the entire deck over and over again and this is fine for some. But for others, it is better to break the deck into manageable chunks and then learn each one individually. A chunk could be a single slide or section of the presentation; different people have different amounts of data they can absorb at one time. If you decide that you are best learning one slide at a time, try to also add a means of memorising what slide comes next on each occasion. This will enable you to make smoother, more professional transitions from one slide to the next.

A number of TV personalities rehearse every little aspect of their performance, right down to what you and I would consider to be errors – actually they are staged mistakes. Sometimes you will see a person perform live, such as a famous comedian and then when you buy the DVD from a different venue, you'll spot the exact same apparent slip ups. It's all down to meticulous rehearsal.

As you get to the stage in your rehearsal that you really do know your content word perfectly, remember not to lose the style and personality of your presentation. We've seen many examples of the presenter speaking with little or no inflection in their voice and delivering their presentation in a very monotone manner – Word perfect maybe, but not all that engaging. Why not use a simple personal voice recorder to record your own narration just to make sure that you physically sound as engaging as you mentally hope you do?

To summarise rehearsing a presentation, in basic terms, you simply can't do too much of it! The more you get to know your presentation, the more your confidence will grow. That alone should be a good reason to invest in some serious rehearsal time. Secondly, start to develop a strategy for rehearsing and identify what you need to learn and how best you are able to absorb that information. The good thing about rehearsing all or part of a presentation is you can do it almost anywhere: mentally on the bus, while walking the dog, at lunch, even in bed at night. Remember that whenever you attempt to commit specific things to memory, use emotion to more solidly embed the data and catalogue it in a more retrievable way. Finally, place each of the things you want to remember on a journey that is very familiar to you. That way, simply mentally travelling the journey will remind you of those items (and in the correct order). Oh, and although you can't over rehearse, you can over memorise and when you do, you'll find that the style and personality goes out of your key messages; try to memorise emotionally and recollect with just as much emotion and present those key messages with even more feeling.

So it's all well and good that you have thoroughly learnt your presentation, but ask yourself this: What if you've learnt the wrong thing? What we mean is, what if there is an error in your presentation? In the next chapter, we'll urge you to employ the help of others as you hone and fine tune your masterpiece.

Get a second opinion

"The only man who never makes a mistake is the man who never does anything."
Theodore Roosevelt

Audiences love errors on screen: they seek them out, they hunt them down and they like nothing more than pointing them out during the actual event. This frustrating aspect of human behaviour does little to benefit the presentation; it hits the confidence of the presenter and undermines the credibility of their content for starters. So the best way to avoid such a situation is to thoroughly check, double check and review the presentation before the big event.

When it comes to reviewing your presentation draft sometime before the big day, then there's a well-worn phrase worthy of mentioning here: Two heads are better than one. To begin with, let's consider the aspect of proofreading and data checking. There's no foolproof formula for perfect proofreading; as it's just too tempting to see what we meant to write rather than the words that actually appear on the page or screen (but there won't be too many words on the screen anyway... will there?). The first purpose of your assistant proofreader is to listen to your presentation as you deliver it (including comparing what you say with what is on the screen). Better still, get them to present it to you and to read out any of your speaker notes to you. This way you'll have a chance to hear what the audience is intended to hear and so pick up any possible errors in relation to the combination of patter and on-screen content.

Secondly, you and your accomplice should both double-check facts, figures, and even proper names. Ask your assistant to point out anything they don't quite understand and then make sure that it really does make sense (remember we see what we mean, not the words as they appear). The more familiar you are with a presentation, the less you are able to read it word for word and data point by data point. Your brain will override your desire for accuracy in favour of efficiency.

When going through your presentation and checking data go the extra mile and also make sure you do your history. If you refer to items in the news, make sure they are still currently accurate. When talking of businesses, check that they haven't changed their name. In particular, if using pictorial logos, spend time ensuring that they are the most up-to-date version. We recently heard of a supplier pitching for a major business contract from one of the world's leading food manufacturing organisations. They had the best offer, the most compelling presentation, but lost out on the pitch. Why? Because they used the potential customer's logo that had been changed some 18 months earlier (and significantly altered too). In essence, the supplier had demonstrated to this important possible client that their attention to detail wasn't all that hot, and it was that which cost them the business.

Another technique for checking the detail in your presentation is to review a hard copy. Print out your text and review it word by word and number by number. The exercise of rereading your work in a different format can help you pick up errors that you'd previously missed. Incidentally, this way of checking can be enhanced by reading your presentation backwards; by starting at the last word on the final slide.

Watch out for those apparently timesaving ways of saving time whilst creating a presentation that can trip you up. For example, if relying on just the spell checker to pick up errors in your deck, then remember that American English and International English are very different languages, both in terms of pronunciation and spelling (realise, realize, for example). Check to see if you are using the correct dictionary for your spell checking. This leads on to the matter of who the spelling should be correct for. Imagine you are an American presenting to a room full of British students – Here, you should aim to spell things as they would do (International English). It isn't too serious if you decide to retain the American spelling, it just means that their attention will be interrupted somewhat and subsequently the communication effectiveness weakened. Whichever spelling option you select, don't mix and match as this can look unprofessional and again sends out a perception of a lack of attention to detail.

If you are prone to make the same errors when typing (such as mistyping its and it's), then take time to review the presentation and to look for them individually. In this example, go through your presentation and just concentrate on checking each time its or it's appears.

Finally on checking for errors, pay particular attention to images as they can contain a wealth of incriminating evidence. For example, helping yourself to a stock photo off the Internet without paying the royalty may result in your audience seeing the watermark in the image and questioning your trustworthiness. These online thumbnails often have watermarks to prevent others using them without paying for them. Another common error is to horizontally flip an image so that the design of the slide looks more balanced. Flipping this way means creating a mirror image and is created by dragging the left handle of the image across past the right side. Although this results in a more balanced slide layout, any words on the image will now be backwards and if the words are in the background of the image, they can easily be missed.

The most thorough way of having your presentation checked before the main event is to have it done so professionally. Presentation consultants are well worth the investment because they can not merely enhance the presentation itself, but they also check for errors and they do so from an entirely neutral perspective. An objection some people have to this service is that it costs money. We prefer to think of it this way – If the presentation content either costs money to obtain or is aimed at attracting money (selling something), then compare the potential amounts with the likely cost of ensuring the optimal delivery. In other words, consider the value of the presentation professional, not only the cost.

In summary, when it comes to error and accuracy checking your presentation, spend time and effort and ask others for help. The more polished the final presentation, the more memorable the key messages will be, and for the right reasons.

Now, it's fair to say that however much we try, things will go wrong. We may forget, something may occur out of our control or there may be the notorious system malfunction along the way. For these reasons (and others) the next chapter offers practical advice related to damage limitation and risk management.

Safety nets – A script somewhere, prompts and a back up

"Blessed are the forgetful: for they get the better even of their blunders."
Friedrich Nietzsche

When all is said and done, one of the main problems people face in relation to giving a presentation is simply their own fear. Furthermore, analysis of these fears often reveals one of the root causes as being afraid of forgetting their words or even corpsing. So in this next section, we'll explore some subtle (and not so subtle) methods that the presenter can use to help them both in terms of not forgetting their words but also in reducing their fear.

If you follow the advice given in this book the odds of you ever forgetting your words will be dramatically reduced. But here are some proven techniques to help. Firstly, write your script in the notes section below each slide in PowerPoint (look for a box that says 'Click to add notes'). Then simply print off the presentation in 'Notes Pages' format and have them with you on stage. The key here is to keep them synchronised. That is to say, keep the uppermost of the printed pages the same as the slide on screen. This way, you only have to glance down to see what to say next as opposed to having to spend time flicking through a paper version of your deck. Another trick you can use is to employ the services of an assistant. First, provide them with a set of your notes and ask that they keep them synchronised with the screen. Then, at any point where you need a prompt, they can either show you the page (if they are close enough), hand you the notes or verbally prompt you as to what to say.

If you use Notes Pages in PowerPoint, it's often wise to give a thought to how you lay out the text on them. For example, you really don't want to add every word you will say in long paragraphs of text; this makes it hard to tell at a glance precisely where you are in the text. It's often better to write the notes as bullet points (yes there is a place for bullet points in PowerPoint, but just not on the main screen). In addition, it's useful to have the key word or couple of words in each point in bold so that they stand out more.

Once you have your notes prepared, you can then decide how best to use them on stage. Be careful if holding them in your hand that you don't start literally reading from them, as this is a sure-fire means of disengaging the audience. Another consideration if you are holding your notes is that if you are shaking, even slightly, then this will be exaggerated by the notes and so more visible to the audience. For the more technically advanced and wealthy presenters, a recent alternative to holding pages of notes is to use an iPad (other tablets are available), but you need to decide how best to advance your electronic notes along with the main presentation screens you're showing to the audience. Using a tablet like this looks both professional and technical. The anchor presenter of BBC1's Formula One motor racing coverage, amongst others, adopted this technique to good effect in 2011.

Sometimes, the presenter is only afraid of forgetting their words when talking about a particular slide. In this case, the previous techniques can be used but only create and use notes for that slide.

Here's another neat trick that helps the Power Presentation flow that little bit more professionally. On the screen itself, but discreetly in a corner, have a small image of the next slide or just the title of it. This will keep you as the presenter more aware of what is coming next and so you can more seamlessly flow from one slide to the next. On the same subject, relating to what else to show on screen, slide numbers are useful as they help you and any assistant you have to keep track of where in the show you are. It also makes it easier to synchronise printed notes with the on-screen material. A word of caution, just because PowerPoint allows you to automatically insert numbers, please don't be tempted to use that all too common format of showing 'Slide 24 of 287'. Because when an audience can see that there are lots and lots more to come, in the majority of cases they will lose interest and mentally disengage. Better to just have the number of the slide and use it only as a prompt for you (and any assistant).

If you want to insert the date, then that's fine, but before you go cluttering up the screen, ask yourself what purpose any content serves. If you can't think of an audience-related one, then as a rule of thumb, don't use it. If you do want to have the date on screen, please make sure that it updates as it's not professional to be presenting something that has on old date clearly visible to all.

As a final safety net, it's always a good idea to have more than a single electronic copy of your presentation with you. For example, if your honed masterpiece is on your laptop, we suggest you have a separate copy on a memory stick. This way, if anything happens to said laptop (and it sometimes does), you have a back up. Conversely, if you are to present on somebody else's computer, using your presentation on a memory stick, you should have a spare copy with you either on another memory stick or on a laptop.

So to summarise this section, as a Power Presenter try to be prepared for as many eventualities as possible. Create access to your notes, by printing them off and concealing them on stage and consider and be prepared to use an assistant if that helps. Finally, give thought to any on-screen prompts; cues as to what is coming next are useful, often more so than filling the screen with more irrelevant details such as the date and the file location of that particular presentation.

Following on from this chapter, ask yourself another question. Do you have a backup plan? The next chapter offers advice regarding possible options you should consider.

What backup plan do I have?

"If you assume something won't go wrong, then it surely will come presentation time."
Ian Callow

I am sure we have all been at a conference, exhibition or meeting when a presenter arrives and things do not go to plan with regard to equipment working. They spend the next five to ten minutes scrambling around on the floor, with various cables in their hand. Perhaps they have arrived and their USB stick containing a key presentation might not be recognised or CD drives may be locked down for network security. These two examples are particularly relevant when presenting on Ministry of Defence bases or other government and high security facilities where network security has to be of the highest level. So that it is not you scrambling around on the floor, the question has to be asked prior to a presentation, what backup plan do I have?

To answer that question we have to ascertain what can malfunction at conference venues or offices and what can be done to eliminate or minimise the impact they will have on our presentation. Remember the presentation you are giving has to be the stand-out feature, not what went wrong in setting up or during the presentation. This can be broken down into two areas: those within our control as a presenter and those outside our immediate sphere of influence. Some areas will cross over but these two areas will form the initial focal point.

Most issues can start to be minimised by consulting with the venue ahead of the presentation. In this case the conference organiser is probably not the best contact as technical specifications will be required regarding computer access, login password, WiFi codes and versions of software installed on a host computer. As a presenter the questions you need to ask of a venue are:

- Does the venue have a host computer?

- If the computer has a USB port is that port only available for encrypted devices?

- Does the host computer have a CD-ROM drive? If so, is the drive unlocked for CDRs?

- Does the host computer have specific login access, especially if the computer goes into screensaver mode?

- Is there a WiFi network available? If so, what are the codes allowing my computer access?

- Which versions of software are on the host computer?

- Is a technician going to be sitting in on the presentation or at least nearby?

With these questions asked and answers hopefully obtained you still better have a backup plan. In all our years of presenting and training, the one item we never rely on is the host computer. Whilst it is the easy option to use the client's computer, always have your own as a backup. Another reason to use your own computer is that you will be familiar with the speed of the processor for loading images and text as required.

With many different ways of transporting media such as USB, CD-ROM and Cloud Computing, having a couple of these for backup is essential. On many occasions I have used Internet storage programs such as Dropbox, which allows quick and easy access of files at clients' offices. All of these elements are within our control, should one area go awry you should be confident in having the backup available.

The real backup plans need to be incorporated when actions outside our control take over the presentation. How do you still get your message across to clients or conference delegates if you are not able to finish or even start your presentation?

Some presentation areas of failure could be projector failure, fire alarms going off, some key person being sick or absent from their post and equipment failure such as the microphone failing midway through the presentation.

All of the above have happened to us at some time or other, the question is how to adapt and react to the situation. Especially when training. For many years within education the fire alarm was a constant issue, particularly in September when new pupils were in school and fire regulations needed to be met. The fire alarm would sound and everybody traipsed out onto a wet and muddy field, all thinking 'why now?' Normally in these circumstances time is of the essence, as further meetings may be scheduled by the clients. This leaves little or no time on that particular date to perform the presentation. You hope that clients would rearrange the presentation; however be prepared to leave behind some form of key reminder. This could be a USB stick with notes, in which case a follow up under these circumstances would be essential.

Speaking at a conference or exhibition, the hardware for presentations is usually supplied by a staging company; this should mean technicians on site who are able to sort all issues. A backup plan should still be available. If microphones or projectors break, how do you react? Whilst you can still talk through the presentation, the impact will probably not be the same as seeing the planned presentation. Notes should be made available to all delegates – remember notes should not be a print out of the slides. Notes should be treated as an individual item in their own right. An alternative solution would be to point delegates to your company website, where your presentation would be made available. An extension of this would be to have a video of you presenting; this allows all of the gestures and body motion to carry the impact as designed into the presentation.

When presenting at a venue off-site from your usual environment clarification needs to be achieved on what is available at the venue and any restrictions that are in place with regard to computer safety. As a presenter you should not assume that the host system will allow the simple plug and play of a USB device carrying your well-crafted presentation. Backup solutions will need to be in place to achieve a smooth running to your own presentation. This preparation is all intended to reduce your nerves at the venue, which allows you to concentrate on your presentation 100%.

Wherever you are asked to present always ask the organiser the question of computer network security. In my experience, military bases, the banking sector, healthcare or large service industries all have secure networks where USB security is enabled. Users have to have password clearance or use encrypted USB devices to allow access to working elements of the computer. Even then, changes to program files are still locked, requiring a remote administrator for access before files can be uploaded.

If your presentation requires the use of a particular piece of bespoke software make sure ample notice is given to the company or establishment, as your software may need clearance to be loaded onto a secure system. In some cases this clearance can take several working days to achieve, or even longer.

One solution is to email your presentation to the conference or meeting organiser ahead of the scheduled date. This though carries a certain level of risk as far as you the presenter is concerned. The first risk is that no last minute changes to the presentation can be included. If market forces change then these have to be excluded or included but purely as a narrative, which certainly does not carry the same impact as visual stimuli. Secondly, the company may look through the presentation ahead of your arrival as part of the vetting process. To avoid any chance of this happening make sure your presentation is password protected. The only addition to making that choice is to let a colleague know the password should illness strike on presentation day; by doing this a last minute substitute presenter is not left floundering at what would probably be a nervous time anyway.

Online storage facilities are becoming standard practice now; companies such as Dropbox and Carbonite allow secure storage and remote access to files. These systems are an ideal solution for sharing files, at the same time allowing the flexibility required to bypass carrying a USB drive in the briefcase or attached to a key ring, or leaving data in a host computer. It is important though, not to rely 100% on this as a solution when visiting external companies. Particularly within the military, Internet access is strictly controlled. Simply accessing the Internet becomes an issue, let alone downloading files from a remote site and installing. This is why preparation ahead of the presentation is required to achieve the full level and clarity required, thus avoiding embarrassment when arriving at a venue.

One of the solutions I have used over the years is the trusty CD-ROM. A read only CD created and written with only the required presentation and resources will negate the need for USB requirements and no data can be written to the CD, which satisfies the host computer system and administrators. Presentation rooms will have a host computer in a cupboard with a CD drive incorporated, allowing access for the read-only CD.

When using a client's computer in a secure environment the system will log off promptly if the mouse is not moved or a key pressed.

This may be after as little as one minute. During a presentation where a discussion forms an important element of the proceedings, the movement of the mouse or the pressing of a key will be forgotten. To reinstate the presentation a user name and password are required. Therefore make sure that the person logging you onto the system forms part of the audience. If not, time is lost chasing down technicians or your initial contact at the venue, wasting time and making you look unprofessional. It will also lead to a disjointed presentation allowing the audience's attention to wane, especially if audience members leave the room to check emails. So in this secure environment it is imperative that the venue either issues you with a visitor login, which allows access to only the files you require or the audience includes the key login party.

When asked to present at a venue, be it a corporate office, exhibition arena or a service industry client, never assume that your presentation can be loaded from a USB device. Be sure to clarify with the named contact the specification of the system available and any restrictions that may apply. A locked-down USB computer can be bypassed with read-only CDs or Internet access from online storage sites. Full Internet access would need to be clarified for the latter solution. In all circumstances, always have your own computer available as the last resort. This may mean unplugging a few cables to link up a projector and speakers but then, quite literally, the show can go on.

So in this section we have considered the need to have a backup plan for when presentations do not go exactly to plan. Things will go wrong at certain times; it is how we react to these issues that counts. By having a backup you will minimise the impact and allow a presentation to be remembered for the right reasons. Remember: Plan, plan and re-plan.

One of the causes of things going wrong is sat there looking at you as you present. They are the audience and they have the power (deliberate or more frequently inadvertently) to derail your polished masterpiece. In the next chapter we turn our attention to the subject of audience participation; whether we want it and how to manage it.

Delegate interaction

"Real answers need to be found in dialogue and interaction and, yes, our shared human condition. This means being open to one another instead of simply fighting to maintain a prescribed position."
Malcolm Boyd

So faced with a presentation, a certain amount of feedback is expected from the delegates. This feedback could be part of focus groups, team meetings, or conferences. Gaining strategic feedback is an essential method of developing and implementing key business plans. In this chapter, methods of gaining feedback will be explored depending on the situation in which you will find yourself. The days of paper flipcharts, 'Post-It' notes, dry wipe marker boards and paper flipcharts can be left behind. Productivity in using these older technologies for corporate meetings can be pretty poor, especially when taking into account the time taken to copy the notes up, which in doing so can lose meaning and, importantly, emphasis. For individual planning of presentations, though, 'Post-It' notes do have their place, as Garr Reynolds demonstrates in his book *Presentation Zen*. Each slide of the PowerPoint presentation can be represented by a 'Post-It' whilst in the planning stage. This makes the ordering of ideas extremely straightforward and visual. For this section larger working groups are really the focus, where notes and feedback can be emailed immediately after presentations allowing key actions to be implemented with purpose.

Dry wipe marker boards in meeting rooms have so many restrictions for today's busy meeting environment. Any notes are marooned in one place on the board and lost forever unless a photograph is taken of the board. This may not be as easy as it sounds as any flash from a camera can bleach out large portions of the board with reflected light off the high gloss surface. A much more productive solution for the business environment is the use of interactive whiteboard or plasma overlays, both of which can have supporting software, allowing electronic notes to be taken without any interruption in the flow. SMART Technologies are one of the largest suppliers in the field of these types of interactive devices. Different solutions are available but the key criteria remain the same. During meetings, unlike a dry wipe board where everything is static, electronic whiteboards allow movement of handwritten notes. This automatically opens up the possibility of ordering feedback from focus groups during brainstorming sessions. Any notes can be saved electronically, allowing instant email in PDF format to clients, suppliers or other departments within the company.

The impact of using an electronic whiteboard for note-taking in large conference venues is somewhat reduced. Too many delegates trying to share ideas can lead to confusion, if not controlled; this in turn may lead to a lack of focus from some in the audience. A solution for larger audiences would be to have electronic voting devices. As with interactive whiteboards the market has numerous systems to choose from. One of the easiest to work with due to its seamless integration into PowerPoint is the solution offered by Turning Technologies. Their solution of an integrated PowerPoint Add-In allows current presentations to be brought into the voting fold without any effort from the presenter. As voting slides are inserted into PowerPoint presentations delegates interact through ResponseCards or mobile phone technology. Results from these sessions can be manipulated in Microsoft Excel and emailed directly to clients.

Having this level of delegate interaction really starts to open up the possibilities for the presenter. During this book you will be gaining an understanding of body language, and how to read the audience. By allowing the audience to interact with the presentation it allows them to have a sense of purpose and intimacy with the presentation as a whole. Rather than conveying information from a PowerPoint presentation in one direction, presenter to delegate, using electronic solutions allows for a multi-directional presentation to evolve.

So far, consideration has been given to audience members or colleagues being present in one room. However, in today's global economy that may not always be the case as offices are spread across the country or the world. Other methods of interaction therefore need to be considered. Several video conference solutions exist for sharing desktops during meetings but in this chapter we are really looking to the written feedback for a response. File sharing sites classed as 'The Cloud' do allow documents to be shared and edited by a number of people. Dropbox allows multi-user sharing of folders and documents. If this type of system is used it is worth having a nominated administrator, else files may be moved or annoyingly deleted. Once a document is opened and access granted, any number of delegates can be feeding back directly into the one document. All delegates logged in at that time see the latest notes, which allows interaction from anywhere in the world. This collaborative approach to meetings may take a little time to embed, but the result of increased productivity will outweigh the learning curve experienced.

There is one question that as a presenter you should consider when designing the presentation. Is the use of interactive technology going to enhance the presentation? If you are unsure about the answer to this question then stay away from the technology. Any use of technology must improve the presentation message and productivity of feedback to colleagues. Do not use interactive technology if it is going to detract from the message of the presentation.

This chapter has opened the possibility of being more creative with regard to audience participation. Depending on the venue size, solutions exist to move meetings and presentations into the electronic age, banishing dry wipe boards and paper flipcharts to the scrapheap. Take time to explore the possible interactive solutions outlined; used effectively the image of professionalism shared with the audience can have an extremely positive effect.

Audience participation

"Participation, I think, is one of the best methods of educating."
Tom Glazer

The style and length of a presentation will vary depending on the requirements of the conference organiser and your own requirements as a presenter. During this book, time has been spent considering the attention span of delegates or audience members. And when is the best time to 'hit' the audience with the key message of the presentation? This, as a rule of thumb, is around the five-minute mark.

Consideration needs to be given to presentations that last around 20–25 minutes and how to keep delegates concentrating on the presentation.

During this chapter we will be looking at a selection of methods of asking questions during a presentation and how this will maintain the audience attention, making them feel engaged with the presentation. Having the audience engaged will make the key messages transfer smoothly. We are not talking about putting a single audience member under pressure or making audience members uncomfortable, we are considering group responses.

Different forms of interaction need to be considered from the cheap and easy to the more expensive, but powerful solutions of electronic polling systems. These electronic systems allow key demographic data to be collected – ideal for detailed reporting and product development. The type of participation needs to be reflective of the audience size and the knowledge delegates have of each other. For instance, a question in a small group of work colleagues answered by a show of hands is unlikely to provide a truthful response, especially if negative; peer pressure is far too large an influence. At a conference a show of hands may be an acceptable method of gaining some understanding of the audience's state of mind.

The drawback of the show of hands technique is that all information is lost as soon as the hands are pulled back down. Also, if a poll is close it may be extremely difficult to distinguish between hands, dare I say some delegates may even vote twice using each hand. Incidentally, this can be overcome by introducing a coloured card system, as you know delegates only have one card.

This type of card polling system is sometimes used in television shows. Two examples are *Ready Steady Cook*, a show where audience members vote on the best prepared dish on a cooking show. Red tomatoes and green peppers are used. A second example is on *Chris Moyle's Quiz Night*, a panel game show where audience members are asked to vote on which celebrity will win at the end of the evening. In this case the face of each celebrity taking part is held high. In both cases this audience participation adds colour and engages the audience in the show accordingly. As with the show of hands, once the poll is over the information is lost unless some soul has to take a video or camera image of the audience, therefore not ideal.

If the audience is going to be asked questions and interact with a presentation it makes sense to try and keep those responses for later reflection. Using electronic polling devices allows results to be captured and analysed. Many conference organisers now offer some form of electronic polling device as this type of audience participation becomes more mainstream.

One of the best systems, simply because of the interaction with PowerPoint, is a system called TurningPoint as we've already mentioned. Designed as an Add-In to PowerPoint the software allows a presentation to flow seamlessly. This seamless movement between an information slide, which conveys the key message, and question slides gauging the audience response, makes for a fully-integrated approach and solution. Information can be anonymous, by participant or even demographic group.

In summary, asking questions of delegates helps to maintain a level of engagement, which allows the key message to be transferred. The easiest solution of showing hands or cards for larger audience sizes provides a ready solution; this though can be extended if electronic polling systems are introduced. The ability to capture data from responses also forms an important solution. This data can be analysed for detailed reporting even if the responses are collected anonymously.

Importantly, the more you can gain from the audience in front of you and still convey those key messages has to be of later benefit. This leads us on to the inevitable subject of question and answer sessions. In the next chapter, we'll discuss the pros and cons and also offer advice regarding how you can tilt their effectiveness in your favour.

When allowing questions and answers

"In examinations, the foolish ask questions the wise cannot answer."
Oscar Wilde

When to allow questions is an interesting area and views will vary depending on the presenter and their particular style. Also, the content of a presentation will lead to different solutions. To answer the question, consideration will be given as a guide for your own development with some essential points in becoming a Power Presenter.

When running training sessions we make it quite clear to delegates that they are free to ask questions at anytime during the session. We would rather have this scenario then have a delegate thinking of the question for a long time, afraid to ask in case it annoyed us, the trainers, or the other delegates. Constricting the question time can have a negative effect on two fronts. Firstly, the delegate may not concentrate on other important elements if their mind is still dwelling on a point from ten minutes ago. Secondly, they may forget the question and only remember when they have left the room and you have left the building. One has to be careful though not to let a single alpha male or female delegate hog the limelight and ask too many questions as this will prove to be disruptive.

When answering a question in a training session we apply a simple rule of thumb – If we are going to cover the ground that will answer the question later on in the session then we will park the question and let the delegate know that we will answer that particular question during that period. If the question asked is relevant to the current topic then we will answer to the best of our ability.

This understanding works well in the training environment. The presentation environment requires a slightly modified approach due to the nature of PowerPoint and the message you have prepared. The message that you have prepared should answer the majority of questions delegates may ask, purely through your anticipation and understanding of the subject matter. Anticipating questions that will be asked also allows delegates to maintain a high level of engagement with the presentation.

For a PowerPoint presentation it is good practice to have designated times when questions can be asked. These times should be made clear to delegates at the outset of the presentation, so they have clarity in their own minds. Question sessions are ideally stationed at specific chapter breaks in a presentation, especially if the presentation is over, say, a 15-minute time period. This would allow the audience to gain breath from the focused information, at the same time creating the clarity required to send the audience home satisfied. For shorter presentations, questions during the presentation are an unrealistic expectation of the audience and best saved until you have completed the entire presentation. If your presentation is scheduled to last 10–15 minutes, that time is valuable and timed to perfection through your practice beforehand. Questions during these shorter presentations will simply allow disruption to occur and therefore noise to the overall key messages, so avoid until the end.

When questions are asked by audience members some important rules apply. Firstly, is the question relevant to the presentation? The answer to this is important. If the question raised is not relevant to the presentation then the chances are it is a long term issue that someone is experiencing. This issue should not be discussed in front of the other audience members as it will be of little or no interest to them. This can only distract from the key message of the presentation. If this situation occurs answer the delegate by explaining that you will see them individually after the presentation, allowing more details to be collected.

Secondly, is the question being asked maliciously? Believe it or not, some questions can be asked maliciously, trying to catch the presenter out. This scenario creates a mindset of fear in presenters' minds. Panic can set in if the answer is not known and therefore seen as a sign of weakness. Honesty in these circumstances can be the best policy, explain to the delegate that you don't have the answer to hand but you will contact them with the answer as soon as possible after the presentation.

The third aspect here relates to you respecting the questioner – Never belittle the audience. Your audience are the life of your presentation, carrying it with them when they leave the conference venue. If, when answering questions, the terminology has been of a condescending manner then the key message will be completely forgotten. Therefore, responding to an audience question by telling them it was covered on Slide 3 is not a satisfactory resolution. Careful explanation still needs to be given allowing the audience as a whole to feel inclusive to the presentation. Questions answered with care and understanding will build the confidence of other audience members to ask questions. Questions answered abruptly will kill any question and answer session, and your key presentation message.

Following on from the previous point, try never to argue with an audience member while you are on stage. Just because an audience member asking a question has a different viewpoint, this does not give you right to answer by way of an argumentative tone or stance. Continue a discussion after the presentation over a coffee if points need to be clarified.

Another good tactic to employ during question and answer sessions is to begin your response by repeating the audience member's question. This is important on three fronts: Firstly, it tells the audience member asking the question that you have heard the question correctly; secondly, some audience members may not have heard the original question, especially in large auditoria where microphones may not be available for audience use. This repeating of the question via your presentation microphone involves them in the answer that will be following; finally, repeating the question gives you, the presenter, time to think of an answer, these valuable few seconds can be precious in formulating a coherent reply.

For smaller audiences, repeating the question may not be as important but time still needs to be taken before answering the question – a creative pause. We have mentioned about formulating a reply by repeating the question. A pause before answering will have another effect; it will allow the audience to take stock of the question. This allows the question to be embedded in their memory rather than them being swamped with an immediate answer. These manufactured pauses can be created by taking a sip of water, or having a joke with the audience in relation to the question.

After answering a question from an audience member always acknowledge them at the end of the answer to check that your answer has actually answered their question. Any answers should be kept as concise as possible to avoid rambling answers that will lose focus and integrity. A weak presenter may see the opportunity for a long answer as a way of avoiding further questions.

The point at which questions are asked is open to styling, presentation length and subject matter. Training and presentation environments allow for two different strategies; however the core principles remain the same. Each question asked needs to be interpreted by the presenter and a suitable answer conveyed to the audience member asking the question. This answer may have to follow on if the answer is not fully known at the venue. As a presenter, do not be afraid of acknowledging that you do not know the answer; better this than trying to bluff your way to an incorrect answer. Your integrity in the minds of the audience must remain intact for them to carry your key message out of the conference venue. This integrity is maintained by answering questions honestly, without belittling or arguing with audience members.

Above all, questions should be encouraged but one rule still applies. Never finish a presentation on a question and answer session. Once all questions are asked, take a few minutes to thank the audience; at the same time reviewing the key points of the presentation so it is fresh in their memory.

Let's now move on to the subject of 'planted questions'. Your presentation has finished and there is a pause for questions, that pause extends and extends some more. If you are not careful, this extended pause can be detrimental to the presentation, as both you and your delegates may start to feel uncomfortable and this becomes the lasting memory. Whilst as a Power Presenter you should not be afraid of a certain level of silence, as it brings valuable thinking time, an extended pause should be avoided. These extended pauses can be avoided with a small amount of planning. For example, a good way to kick off a Q and A session is to use planted questions – getting people you know to ask about things you were aware of in advance. This settles any trepidation you may have and enhances your persona. It also gives the audience time to think of questions they want an answer to. In addition, it's funny how so few audience members want to be the first to ask a question and this circumvents that conservatism and hesitation.

One of the key stages to a successful question and answer session is to make the audience as relaxed as possible. If an audience feels intimidated following the presentation, questions will be hard to come by. This intimidation could be generated by a presentation pitched at too high a level; an audience bombarded with irrelevant information will build an imaginary barrier to the presenter and presentation. This is why the presentation needs to be adapted for a variety of audiences; simply basing a presentation on one fixed narration will lead a presenter into a false sense of security.

Relaxing the audience not only comes from the quality of the presentation on screen, it also comes from you the presenter. A taut, rigid stance will convey a sense of tension to the audience, whilst a softened stance with slightly bent knees and open arms will generate a sense of control and relaxation. The same importance can be applied to the tonal quality of the voice. A softly spoken presenter can be a sign of nerves, therefore it is important to project the voice whilst looking at the audience and not to the floor of the stage.

Section 3 – Your Performance: Summary

"An ounce of performance is worth pounds of promises."
Mae West

As we come to the end of Section 3, we've learnt much about being a Power Presenter, creating a Power Presentation and now delivering it. In this section specifically, we learnt that when your presentation is part of a larger event, it's always advisable to check for duplication of content or, worse still, direct contradiction. Has somebody (perhaps the event organiser) checked that the presentations do in fact work together? As well as checking for contradictions, avoid yourself and others saying the same thing, particularly if this involves using the same data sources, video clips and examples. Your presentation should be unique within the event, but designed to work as an integral part of it.

When it comes to working with any other speakers presenting, the first tool you can use is to reference their key messages in your own presentation. With regard to competitive presentation situations, remember to never criticise your competitors. Wiser to help the audience to come to the conclusion that you are better than your competitors rather than telling them.

As you deliver your crafted masterpiece (ergo, you perform), remember that just as individual slides make up part of a presentation and should flow from one to another in a logical and understandable order, then so do presentations link together to become an event.

On occasions when you are the only presenter and not part of any larger event, you need to adopt a significantly different approach. Being the only presenter involves managing more of the audience attention mindset. The first thing you need to do is get their attention and we explored a number of techniques for achieving just this objective.

What about the aspect of when you present? In this chapter we highlighted the importance of recognising and asking the question, "When was the last break for delegates and when will be the next one?" Only once you know the answers to these questions can you tailor your presentation style and tone to generate or regenerate audience attention and engagement to optimal effect. When accepting an invitation to present, be fully aware of when delegates had their last break. Presenting when delegates have being sitting down for an hour is not conducive to a successful presentation and so should be avoided. Presenting immediately after a coffee break provides the opportunity to mingle with delegates, creating a bond with the audience prior to your performance. All delegates will be refreshed, avoiding the influence of fidgets on your presentation. Following these guidelines will provide you, the budding Power Presenter, with a head start when organising your conference presentation slot.

We then went on to discuss just how the orientation of the venue can have a direct impact on your performance. If the orientation is right then delegates are more likely to absorb the information coming their way; get the orientation wrong and messages can be lost in the discomfort delegates may be feeling. The configuration and orientation of the room may also be different from the environment that all of your practice took part in; this could lead to increasing any nerves you may be experiencing prior to the presentation.

As a Power Presenter, your performance can benefit from numerous aspects of attention to detail and next we covered how much freedom you have to present and how much you can mingle with the audience. For example, if you present from the stage, that will demonstrate to the audience a certain level of control in guiding the slide transitions with body gestures whilst showing a calm exterior. Avoid presenting from behind a lectern as this option builds a barrier to the audience and a restriction for transmitting the key messages to delegates.

Talking of delegates, how well do you know them? Those that you know personally in an audience need to be treated as any other delegate before and during the presentation. In other words, don't appear too matey, matey. Spending too much time with those you know will not allow you to engage with unknown delegates ahead of the presentation. The unknown delegates need to be acknowledged and you can do this by fine tuning your presentation with regard to dialogue and head movement. Those delegates that you know well will provide an ideal opportunity to initiate the question and answer session as well as give feedback on the presentation as a whole.

We then discussed the topic of movement in relation to your presentation performance. We explored some basic dos and don'ts relating to how you should stand in front of an audience, including not overacting (exaggerated body movements and gestures) and having the confidence to relax and move around the stage. Remember, our inner mental state often reflects our physiological poise, so you need to physically present yourself as you want to feel. Secondly here, don't be rooted to the spot; you will appear much more engaging to the audience if you move around the stage – own it and use it accordingly. By moving around, you are giving yourself the opportunity of appearing to engage more with those watching you and also, you can use the movement to great effect to add emphasis to points you are making as you present.

As we mentioned in the next chapter, it is also important for you to pay attention to where you look as you present. Over and above making sure to engage with as many parts of the room and audience members as possible, you should endeavour to use your own direction of gaze to direct where you want the audience to look. Even when designing slides, understand how and where humans are most and least likely to look and then create your presentations with this in mind.

Other considerations with regard to where the presenter should look while they present include not simply reading a script; rather, engage with different areas of the audience and manage when you want their visual attention on the screen. Also, as you are looking out at the audience, remember to frequently inspect how engaged they appear to be with your presentation and be prepared to act on the instant visual feedback you receive.

While on the subject of where the audience looks we then went on to reveal how your location in relation to the screen on stage has a direct relationship with the propensity of the audience to view it and their level of engagement as they do. In the western world, people read from left to right and the same is true when they look at a PowerPoint screen. So as a Power Presenter, if you stand on the left of the screen (as the audience sees you), you are then able to make comments and feed in the screen content in a way most naturally for the audience to mentally absorb.

So at this stage we introduced the art of presenter and content working seamlessly together in order to deliver an engaging and memorable performance. Dual encoding is a technique that has been shown to be significantly more powerful than singular verbal or visual encoding. The use of dual encoding helps information pass through into long term memory by creating, firstly, a more multi-sensory related and, ergo, emotional piece of information; and secondly, because the learner creates multiple retrieval routes to the same piece of information.

Another benefit of employing dual encoding is that as you become more accustomed to incorporating dual encoding into your presentation design, you'll find that you are unable to use bullet points on the screen to any beneficial effect; good!

In the next chapter, we revealed the second most important financial investment you can make as a Power Presenter (naturally the most important being in buying a copy of this book!). If you want to deliver a truly memorable, engaging and professional presentation, not only do you need the right presentation but you also need the right tools of the trade. One of these tools is a wireless presentation remote clicker – a small handheld device that gives you direct control of presentation navigation. These relatively low cost devices that are conveniently portable and easy-to-use free you from the single location of the lectern or controlling laptop and relieve you of distraction. They also allow you to focus on what matters most; your Power Presentation.

We then revealed another presenting secret that is used too infrequently – Silence; specifically between slides within a presentation. Surprisingly, for some, pausing is a great way to help both the presenter and the audience. By stopping for just a few seconds, you allow all in the room to metaphorically catch their breath and more effectively embed messages. This also gives you time to collect yourself and prepare to unfold the story on the next slide.

Then we offered a shortcut to presentation excellence for all of you that simply don't have the time to invest in learning all the recommendations, tools and techniques in this book. Namely, watch professional presenters at work: presenters of TV documentaries, weather girls and boys, newscasters and the like. Recognise the techniques that they have spent months and years honing to perfection that you can go right ahead and copy, plagiarise, steal or 'borrow'. It isn't only TV presenters that you can learn presenting skills from. A lot of the world's greatest presentations are captured and then made available on *YouTube* and we recommend that you investigate.

Next, we moved on to the unavoidable, single most important thing you can do to improve your presentation – Rehearse. The more you know your presentation, the greater your confidence will be when it comes to delivering it. In addition, the better prepared you are in terms of knowing your content matter, the less of your brain you have to employ to recall it and so the more mental effort you can assign to the delivery of said information.

We also pointed out that you shouldn't be the sole judge of your content and/or presentation excellence and that whenever possible, you should get a second opinion. Why? Because audiences love errors on screen; they seek them out, they hunt them down and they like nothing more than pointing them out during the actual event. The best way to avoid such a situation is to thoroughly check, double-check and review the presentation before the big event, and a great way to do this is to have someone else help you (more objective and less prone to miss errors). The more polished the final presentation, the more memorable the key messages will be, for the right reasons.

Next, we advocated preparation, and in particular being ready for as many eventualities as possible. Create access to your notes by printing them off and concealing them on stage, and consider and be prepared to use an assistant if that helps. Finally, give thought to any on-screen prompts – Cues as to what is coming next are useful, often more so then filling the screen with more irrelevant details such as the date and the file location of that particular presentation.

Then we considered the need to have a backup plan for when presentations do not go exactly to plan. Things will go wrong at certain times; it is how we react to these issues that matters. Having a backup will minimise the impact and allow a presentation to be remembered for the right reasons. So in summary, rehearse, prepare and have a backup plan.

The book then reverted back to the more positive aspects of the presentation performance and highlighted the importance of highlighting itself, drawing attention to and from particular aspects and points within your presentation. We explored ways you can attract attention to key messages and divert the audience away from specific points. The key being to recognise that you can and need to manage the attention of those you are presenting to. That way, more of them will leave the event thinking precisely what you want them to think.

In the next chapter, we looked at what is in our opinion, one of the most under-recognised golden nuggets any Power Presenter could ever wish to know. The fact that the words spoken by the presenter can represent as little as 7% of what they are communicating at that moment. The words you utter are a core communications tool. However, they are just the tip of the iceberg in terms of what you are communicating with the audience and how effectively you can impart information on them. As you develop as a Power Presenter, use the screen content to add emphasis and 'colour' to what you are saying. Then bring your tone of voice to the fore and recognise how much more effectively you can underscore your key messages.

Don't forget that thing that is responsible for 55% of the feelings and attitude you are communicating – your body. Pay particular attention to your body language to make sure your physiology is congruent with your message. In addition, look at your own facial expressions with a view of beginning to be able to use them as another level of communication support for your presentation message.

Next, the art of two-way communication and asking questions of your audience and how it helps to maintain a level of engagement, which allows the key messages to be transferred. The easiest solution of showing hands or cards for larger audience sizes provides a ready solution; this, though, can be extended if electronic polling systems are introduced. The ability to capture data from responses also forms an important solution. The more information you can gain from the audience in front of you while still conveying those key messages, the greater benefit it will hold for you, the Power Presenter, once the presentation has finished.

Finally in this section, we looked at questions from the audience. When to allow them is an interesting area and views vary depending on the presenter and their particular style. There really is no right and wrong with regard to questions and answers, but as we discussed, there are things you can do to improve your performance. Firstly, decide whether the question is relevant to the presentation and if not, simply say so and move on. Secondly, check whether the question is being asked maliciously (to catch the presenter out) and if so, a safe option is to explain to the delegate that you don't have the answer to hand but you will contact them with the answer as soon as possible after the presentation.

When dealing with audience questions, try never to talk down to the audience and take great care before arguing with them. In the case of the former, always respect the questions, however inane they sound; and with regard to the second, continue the discussion 'off line' in a less public forum if needs be.

Finally, don't be afraid to have planted questions asked by people you know to kick off a question and answer session. By planted, we mean that you are aware of the question and the answer before the event. This settles any trepidation you may have and enhances your persona. It also gives the audience time to think of questions they want an answer to. In addition, it's funny how so few audience members want to be the first to ask a question and this circumvents that conservatism and hesitation.

Section 4

Final thoughts

Section 4 – Final thoughts: Introduction

"Perfection has to do with the end product, but excellence has to do with the process."

Jerry Moran

Well that's almost all there is to changing you from a presenter, to a good presenter, to an excellent one, and to a Power Presenter. Almost, yes. But absolutely everything? No, not quite. In this final section we're going to look at various aspects related to reviewing and analysing each presentation you give as part of your development as a presenter.

Firstly, ask yourself a simple question: "Would you sit through your own presentation?" We have all sat through good presentations. We have all sat through poor presentations. We have all sat through a presentation and wondered how it ever got off the drawing board. We all find it easy to criticise other presenters and their presentations; then pause for a moment and ask the question posed at the beginning of this paragraph.

In the first chapter of this section we explore simple ways that you can use to analyse your own presentation, from recruiting the help of colleagues to the use of electronic aids such as video cameras and the like.

Next we move on to discuss what happens immediately after you deliver your presentation and why you shouldn't file it away as a 'job well done'. If you are committed to being the absolutely best presenter you can, then you need to continually learn and develop. And here we offer some techniques you may wish to employ (we strongly advise you to use at least one of them). We cover self-analysis, employing the services of a friend or colleague and even ways in which you can get professional analysis. Remember, it's all about you having the courage and determination to be the best presenter that you possibly can be. That will drive you to a position whereby you can accept criticism of your presentations. This chapter also offers specific aspects of your presentation to look at, rate and analyse.

In the next chapter, we go even more into the detail and ask readers to do a bit of self-reflection. What did you communicate non-verbally, how did you feel at the time and did this feeling manifest itself in any way, either for good or bad?

Returning back to the different forms of feedback you can utilise, we ask the question, of what feedback do you look for? Do you have any structure for receiving feedback or is it just left to chance? We summarise a number of options you may want to consider.

We can't overemphasize the importance of making your presentation as good as it can be, and if not this one then improve with the next one and so on. All too often, so much hangs on how well the presentation goes and yet presenters seem to think that a few slides loaded with bullet points are enough to do the trick. In our opinion, this should never, ever be the case. In other words, our evidence suggests that the value of the opportunity each presentation offers is all too often severely underestimated, which really is unjustifiable.

In the next chapter we go on to explore how you can receive live feedback actually during your presentation by using a discreet earpiece and again by employing the services of an assistant. Other lower tech ideas are also presented, all aimed at maximising your opportunity while on stage.

The subject of presenter knowledge is discussed in that we explore just how much background knowledge you need to know, and although it differs depending on presentation style and subject, there are some best practice guidelines explained.

Would you yourself sit through the presentation?

"It is especially important to encourage unorthodox thinking when the situation is critical: At such moments every new word and fresh thought is more precious than gold."
Boris Yeltsin

We have all sat through good presentations. We have all sat through poor presentations, as we've already pointed out. We have all sat through a presentation and wondered how it ever got off the drawing board. We all find it easier to criticise other presenters and their presentations than stop and consider this simple question.

It is time to get critical about how you present, and how you present the content within the presentation. Only by having the inner belief that self criticism will allow you, the presenter, to improve performance whilst standing on the stage in front of your audience will you really reach your optimal presenting ability. Achieving analysis of your presentation through colleague analysis or more detailed video-based analysis is a great way to objectively understand your own strengths and weaknesses from a presenting perspective.

With the presentation prepared and ready to go, draft in a colleague to perform your presentation for you. This will provide the ideal opportunity to visualise the slides from a distance as the presentation progresses. Once completed, swap roles, allowing your colleague to be freely critical of the presentation. If your colleague is unsure of an element in the presentation, then chances are members of the audience would also be questioning the same element during your main presentation. Be assured that the critical analysis that follows from your colleague will lead to a presentation of focus and clarity.

Alternatively, consider the use of a video camera. This achieves the important element of distance visualisation for both the presentation itself and the gestures made towards the screen and images on the slides. The review process allows critical analysis to take place in private; this is acceptable as long as you allow yourself to be critical.

It is also possible to combine colleague and video analysis, with the use of company intranets. Placing the video in a shared folder would allow a colleague to view and then comment through email.

Alternatively, companies such as iconnect2learn allow comments to be tagged to video, without the need of email attachments. This solution allows training and best practice to be shared throughout a global company, improving efficiency and reducing the need for costly travel expenses. With the use of video technology distance no longer has to be a restriction on professional development.

To become a Power Presenter you must learn to be critical of your own presentation before those sitting through the presentation themselves are critical. Performing detailed analysis will allow you to build a clear and stronger presentation and reinforce the message of rehearse, rehearse and rehearse.

Reflection – Analyse and improve

"Improvement begins with I."
Arnold H. Glasow

You've done it! As you step down from the stage with the sound of the audience's rapturous applause ringing in your ears, you feel an overwhelming sense of job well done (well this is what we all wanted wasn't it?). At this point, you probably want to just bask in your glory, enjoy your celebrity and make the most of now. All the hard work has paid off and your key messages have hit home better than you could have ever imagined. So what happens next?

For the majority of presenters, they'll move on to their next project, meeting, course or whatever. The presentation just given will be duly distributed and filed away somewhere. But if you are a Power Presenter, you'll have taken another course of action; a brave step into the possibility that your presentation wasn't perfect. Unfortunately, rarely, if ever, can it be said that someone gave the perfect presentation. They may have done very well, but just how close to perfect did they get?

If you are committed to being absolutely the best presenter you can, then you need to continually learn and develop. And with that in mind, here are some techniques you may wish to employ (we strongly advise you to use at least one of them).

The simplest form of analysis (apart from the obvious reaction of the audience) is to arm a colleague with a clipboard and notepad and have them note down details of how you presented each slide. They can be provided with some guidelines as to what to look for; such as did the audience engage with each slide, were you looking all round the room, did some of the audience become distracted, etc. You may want to go further and give them specific body language aspects to quantify: Leaning forwards, looking at the screen, making notes and the like. What you are endeavouring to do is have your colleague quantify how effectively the audience engaged with your presentation.

To take this analysis process a stage further, consider taking the even braver step of having your colleague analyse aspects of your presentation content and style. Have them score each slide in terms of how you and the content worked in harmony to truly 'present' the content. Where did you stand? Did you 'own the stage' and attempt to engage different sections of the audience? At this point you need to be open to criticism and ask your accomplice to also look for any bad habits you may be developing. These may include jangling change in your pockets, rocking from one foot to another or starting to speak at a different speed as the slide builds (usually speeding up). If you present regularly and are able to have an associate objectively study your performance, then you may wish to consider entering your results of each presentation into a spreadsheet to study for patterns of behaviour. The aim of this exercise is to find ways to improve your Power Presenting every time you take to the stage.

Another very effective way to improve the way you present is to have a professional presentation consultant at the event to objectively and comprehensively analyse your performance. We ourselves offer such a service and it can be as part of a tailored package. We'll work with the presenter on their presentation content and their presenting techniques. Then we'll analyse their performance on the big day. This can be done on a one-to-one basis or we can work with teams, departments or entire organisations. Our 'Train the Trainer' sessions educate presenters as to how they can analyse each other and then develop as a group.

A final means of presentation analysis involves the use of technology. To begin with, set up a video camera to film you as you present. In addition, and if you have the resources (and Data Protection Act authority), set up another camera to film the audience.

Once you have the event on film, you have a couple of options. Either you can watch it yourself and analyse how the performance really went. Again, try to do this both objectively and quantitatively. Otherwise, you can send the film to us for our interpretation of your presentation. We'll then undertake a thorough analysis of your performance and submit the findings back to you either as a summary report or in person.

If you're uncertain about which option to choose, then in our experience, a pattern has emerged. Typically, presenters begin by either asking their friend or colleague to analyse them (at a somewhat superficial level). Then, as the confidence and ability rises, they tend to film themselves and see for themselves how good they are. As a third and final step, usually when they think they are proficient presenters to say the least, they arrange to film their performance or have a member of our expert team in the audience.

We can't overstate how important it is for you to monitor and analyse what you are good at when presenting and the areas that need improvement. By doing so, you then recognise which aspects you need to work on and so that subsequently during your rehearsals you can start to really focus on the specifics. There is a good quote attributed to legendary golfer Gary Player (and others if you Google it) who, after sinking a monster putt and hearing a lady in the crowd say, "That was a lucky shot!", responded with, "Well, ma'am, the more I practise, the luckier I get!" The same can be said for Power Presenting, but the key is to recognise and have a structure with regard to what it is that you practise and rehearse and what you are attempting to learn and change.

In summary, just as attention to detail and rehearsal are vital components of good presenting, so is post-presentation analysis. Knowing how the last event went is one thing, but making the next one even better is a whole new ball game. In fact, you could say that the first step towards your next Power Presentation is reviewing and analysing the delivery of your last one.

Self reflection

"Without reflection, we go blindly on our way, creating more unintended consequences, and failing to achieve anything useful."
Margaret J. Wheatley

Various sections of this book have highlighted the importance of self reflection and how this will lead to a more focused and inspired presentation. It is time to explore in greater depth the reasoning why self reflection is so important, and methods of achieving the quality feedback required to improve performance when standing centre stage, preparing to present that key corporate message.

Firstly, a look as to why self reflection is such an important element when preparing a PowerPoint presentation. When we are presenting, any insecurity shown will be conveyed to the audience, thus allowing the message of the presentation to be lost. Even though our presentation slides are dynamic in design and of a high quality this conveyance of nervousness needs to be controlled.

Example indicators that you are presenting with nerves are:

- Arms folded across your chest.

- A rub of the nose every few sentences.

- Both hands in trouser pockets.

- Looking down whilst talking.

- A fidgeting appearance.

- A shallow voice tone.

All of these need to be overcome when becoming a Power Presenter, this is where the importance of self reflection is evident.

We can achieve self reflection either as individuals, with the help of colleagues or by employing mentors to guide you through the self reflection process. The merits of each channel will be developed; the method of each presenter will undoubtedly depend on your own style, working environment and attitude. The process of self reflection is not just limited to the end of the presentation, it is equally important to ensure your presentation is performed to the best of your ability before standing on the stage. This will ensure that the need for those prepared safety nets will not be called upon.

Unfortunately, individual self reflection can be like waving a finger in the air as if checking the direction of the wind, unless the correct tools are applied. The issue of individual self reflection is having a precise understanding of how all of the movements and auditory stimulants were performed:

- Just how did the tone of voice vary?

- Were gestures timed to the slides?

- Did I have any twitches?

- Did I stumble any words?

- Did I look out into the audience?

If your preparation solely involves practising the presentation again and again, this will not eliminate all bad habits, as firstly, you need to clearly understand what your bad habits are. These questions will all be answered if the presentation was captured on video. Whilst this is not necessarily practical at all venues and presentations performed, it certainly is practical and essential when rehearsing the presentation back at the office. To understand how your presentation is progressing, video and review, then video and review again. This will not only generate confidence internally but allow those important external gestures to be honed ahead of the presentation. Remember, gestures do not need to be overly exuberant; if they are it will cause a distraction for the audience and the message of the presentation will be lost.

The next concept of becoming a Power Presenter really pushes the boundaries. Whilst you are presenting and directing individual lines at members of the audience, how are the remainder of the audience reacting? Once you have left the venue that imagery will be forgotten. As a concept, try videoing the audience as you are presenting (Data Protection Act permitting). You will then be able to gauge their reactions as key words and phrases appear in the show. This will provide a clear indication of whether the presentation message is actually getting transmitted to the audience. A basic knowledge of body language applied to the video will provide feedback allowing any actions to be reviewed and improvements to be implemented.

Allowing a colleague to review your presentation both pre and post the scheduled event is an important step on the reflection pathway to success. Be aware though when choosing the colleague, they must have the experience required to guide you as a Power Presenter. Basically, have they reached the level of presenting attainment to which you are aspiring? Being trained by a more inexperienced colleague is not going to enhance your presentation skills. If no colleagues meet this criterion then it is worth considering an external mentor. The support and advice offered would be independent and confidential. With video support this could work as a remote relationship, ideal for multi-site operations.

Remote video analysis across the Internet is available through a company called iconnect2learn (www.iconnect2learn.com). Tagging descriptive comments to video allows the remote mentor to support a client from anywhere in the world. As a presenter it allows you to build a library of best practice for professional development, a key feature for the budding Power Presenter.

Whilst video is an ideal method to use when preparing your presentation, we have already mentioned that it is not always practical at venues. Time restrictions in setting up will be the largest restrictor in pursuing this method of self reflection. It is important to leave the venue with some feedback from delegates. Paper feedback forms just add to the paperwork and are time-consuming, when increasing productivity should be the aim of any presenter. The use of electronic polling devices as mentioned in previous sections provide that immediate feedback without the need to impose on the audience. A few well-selected questions based on a scale of 1 to 5 will give an indication to the audience's feeling about the presentation. Questions such as:

- Did you feel engaged in the presentation?

- Are you clear on what was offered?

- How would you rate the presentation?

- Where you satisfied with the answers to questions?

With this feedback gathered electronically, a report is available immediately.

Finally, use the third way. What is the third way? Working practice has changed over recent years. Many meetings now take place in coffee shops rather than homes or offices. The plethora of shops such as Starbucks, Costa Coffee, Cafe Nero and not forgetting MacDonald's, means analysis of your presentation can begin whilst the presentation is fresh in the mind. Pull off the road and begin the self reflection process. With wireless connectivity in store and many printers having e-print facilities, the final report can be waiting for you when arriving home.

In summary, self reflection is an area not to be avoided, but one that needs to be embraced in becoming a Power Presenter. Whichever method you choose it should form a basic requirement used in conjunction with the principle of rehearse, rehearse and rehearse.

You could go a stage further and encourage feedback from the audience and in the next chapter, we'll look at the types of electronic feedback devices that are available should you want to use them.

Electronic feedback

"Feedback is the breakfast of champions."
Ken Blanchard

So your presentation is over and you are leaving the venue in your car or racing to the station to catch the train currently pulling into the platform. Have you stopped to ask yourself this question? What feedback do you have following the presentation? The answer could be paper evaluations that were collected at the end of the presentation or even how long the applause lasted once your last sentence was completed. Although these may give a certain level of attainment, does it accurately portray the presentation? Not to mention the amount of time for someone back at the office to collate the evaluation sheets.

The use of electronic feedback will give an instant and accurate representation of your presentation. Moreover, electronic feedback does not have to be saved until the end of the presentation; using electronic devices midway through a presentation can guide a presenter to alternative slides. This can be achieved using a form of conditional branching.

Now the scene is set for electronic feedback let us investigate the advantages that are available to a Power Presenter. For corporate industries, information is the key to success. The more detailed the information gained the greater power is available to develop ideas and corporate branding. Brands are established on demographic analysis amongst other psychological and physiological factors. Electronic voting systems allow the gathering of demographic information from delegates through non-obtrusive techniques. How individual members at a conference, or within a focus group, vote will be extracted in the analysis at the end of the presentation. More detail about the analysis of data comes later on in this chapter.

When using PowerPoint to present you are to some extent limited in the navigation between slides, unless a presentation is designed with multiple hyperlinks. Even by using hyperlinks a certain number of slides will need to be shown before moving to a new chapter or section. By including polling into the presentation if a certain level of knowledge or agreement is reached, then the presentation will automatically advance to a different slide than if the level was not met. This allows the presenter to concentrate the presentation on the facts that need to be included. A really important point to introduce is that the same presentation may result in different paths, depending on the feedback. This is important from a presenter's viewpoint as it eliminates the need to constantly change and anticipate how an audience is going to react, allowing the same presentation to be recycled. Having said that, if your presentation needs adapting to meet a higher or lower level of management structure, make sure those focused improvements are followed through.

Now, it has been established that electronic polling systems allow a presenter to focus presentations down to core elements as delegates respond. At the same time demographic information will be collected for later analysis if selected by the presenter. The after-presentation feedback is equally important. Asking a few targeted questions will help in the self-review process explored elsewhere in this book. The collection of data is all well and good but how to present the information is equally important. The polling system used by Turning Technologies allows the information collected during a PowerPoint presentation to be presented in Microsoft Excel with a few clicks of the mouse. As the results are presented in Excel they can therefore be manipulated, saved and emailed to colleagues, meaning increased productivity as no manual result collating is necessary.

What if electronic voting devices are not available to you? This may be the case when presenting at an external conference or exhibition venue. Due to the nature of this type of presentation, a tight schedule does not allow individual evaluation or feedback forms to be distributed and collected. Feedback though is still extremely important. How can this be achieved? If your presentation is designed for a conference then you should leave a certain amount of information as a 'carrot' for delegates. It could be as simple as having prizes online, or setting discounts if resellers sign up to a new incentive. Alternatively, have the presentation notes available through the company website. Having presentation notes available online does not mean simply uploading the PowerPoint presentation. Supporting notes and the presentation are two completely different entities, and so should be treated as such. Microsoft Word is a far more accepted method of presenting detail relating to presentation slides. If you feel slides alone give sufficient detail to be distributed as notes then your presentation needs to be redesigned as it is not designed with the audience in mind. The detail is more than likely acting as a script for the presenter.

The important element is feedback. Directing delegates with some form of incentive to a website, where an online feedback form is available, allows data to be collected. As a presenter in these circumstances an acceptable percentage level of delegate participation needs to be set, as obviously 100% delegate feedback would be unlikely.

In summary, the concept of introducing electronic feedback during and after a presentation will be important in establishing management decisions. The speed at which analysis takes place allows for greater productivity and cost savings throughout a company. Also, having the ability to capture demographic data and move through PowerPoint presentations depending on responses received introduces new concepts in presenting. Online feedback forms introduce the possibility of capturing information, especially where large conference or exhibition presentations have taken place.

With this electronic technology available there is no reason why a presenter cannot gain an insight into what their audience was thinking during a presentation.

Further support – Live advice

"If the impulse to daring and bravery is too fierce and violent, stay it with guidance and instruction."
Xun Zi

Nowadays, so many organisations and individuals rely so much on making commercial gain from delivering a presentation: it may be a sales pitch, credentials presentation or even an entire company strategy. Whatever the case, all too often, so much hangs on how well the presentation goes and yet the presenter seems to think that a few slides loaded with bullet points are enough to do the trick. In our opinion, this should never, ever be the case.

Consider this example. Imagine you are talking at a conference on a particular subject and that your objective is to showcase the abilities of your company to the amassed audience of 100 people. Have you ever stopped to quantify the potential business you could gain from the event and so how much it would be sensible to invest? In our opinion, not enough people do this. Let's imagine that you sell your service for £10,000 and as we said there are 100 people in the room – that means if they all ordered just one, that's £1,000,000 worth of orders from a single presentation (ok so this may seem a bit farfetched). But the point we're trying to make is that the value of the opportunity each presentation offers is all too often severely underestimated. Typically, the presenter is left to create their own presentation (occasionally with some ad hoc assistance) and then to deliver it with as much strategic forethought as is given to deciding whether to 'go large' in the fast food restaurant.

Let's go back to the world of TV, where the art of presenting has been refined and honed over many years. In particular, consider how many people who present live pieces to camera are wearing earpieces – the fact is, a lot of them. And as a professional imparter of information, then why shouldn't you do so too? It is asking a lot to expect the presenter to be able to deliver key messages and analyse the room at the same time to make sure that their presentation is as effective as possible.

Wearing a small earpiece and having a friend or colleague there to offer advice as you present can be a powerful means by which you can optimise your delivery. It can also help in case you are nervous about forgetting your lines by having an audio *aide-mémoire* there at your disposal.

You can make your presentations just that bit more professional by employing some outside direction (having the director communicate in your ear). They can let you know how much time you have spent, how much you have left and whether you are behind or ahead of schedule. They are there in case you have a memory lapse and they can also feedback on the engagement levels of the room. However much you do or don't recognise the benefits of having a second person help you present by advising is up to you, but the low cost of trying this out is certainly worth giving it a go in our opinion.

It is worth noting however, that if you have an earpiece in as you present, you need to instil into the person 'on the other end of the line' not to talk at the same time as you. They should offer advice in times between when you are speaking so as not to confuse you. Some 'double acts' have a tonal code whereby the assistant makes the presenter aware that they want to give advice and the presenter then creates the silent opportunity to do so (such as taking a drink of water).

It may be that you think wearing an earpiece is a step too far for the type or types of presentation you give. There is a lower tech alternative in the form of a personal assistant – someone who is there on hand to follow your presentation and to direct you as you present. They may be there just to make sure you don't 'forget your lines'. Alternatively, their role may be to provide you with live feedback as to how the presentation is going (just as with the earpiece, but using gestures instead of audio). The overriding point is that if there is a potential financial benefit from the presentation, consider the value of it in relation to the cost of creating and delivering the absolutely best presentation possible.

As we've already said, a presenter on television has others to help them and to do some of their thinking as they present; and they may be just reporting on some insignificant regional news event. So surely as a person whose commercial future is entirely or in part reliant on the messages that audiences take from their presentations, consider having a support structure in place, earpiece or otherwise.

A number of presenters we've worked with confuse having a support structure with having every answer to all the questions an audience might ask them. We've known presenters have colleagues at an event sat at data-filled laptops, just in case a member of the audience asks the illusive question they may themselves not be able to answer. Often, this is overkill and does little more than make the presenter feel more at ease. When it comes to scenarios like this we think it is better to be honest with the audience and say that as a presenter you are unlikely to be able to answer every question they may have, but reassure them that you will go away and find the answers they want.

Incidentally, beware the member of the audience intent of making a name for themselves and be armed with a strategy to deal with them. Typically these individuals are assistants or juniors in commercial organisations. They sit and listen to a presentation while at the same time crafting a question that they will ask with the sole intention of making them look good (in their own minds anyway). Sometimes it is the more senior members of an organisation who, resistant to change, try to dig their heels in and ask an awkward question so as to discredit the presenter.

In either of these examples our advice is simple. Once you recognise that the question is being asked not just because the person wants to know the answer (we've all heard such examples at presentations), begin by acknowledging and respecting the question and the questioner, then trip them up! An example of how to do this would be to say something like, "Wow that's a great question. So that I can give you the best answer, either now or later, can you tell me a little more about why you want to know the answer?"

When it comes to having live advice, like many other tactics and strategies related to Power Presenting, it pays to think things through. Does an assistant add value to your presentation? Can they help you more effectively deliver your key messages and how much information must you have to hand to satisfy the reasonable requirements of the audience?

Section 4 – Final thoughts: Summary

"By three methods we may learn wisdom: First, by reflection, which is noblest; second, by imitation, which is easiest; and third by experience, which is the bitterest."
Confucius

Now we really are at the end of a journey. One that we sincerely hope has opened your eyes to just how good a presenter you can be and more importantly, how vital it is to actually deliver quality presentations. We've also seen that delivering quality goes beyond just the information you convey. In fact, Power Presenting is actually a science containing aspects of psychology, physiology, communication and design to name but four.

In this final section, we began by explaining the importance of reviewing and analysing each presentation you give as part of your development as a presenter. We advised readers to get critical about how you present, and how you present the content within the presentation, by having the inner belief that self criticism will allow you, the presenter, to improve performance whilst standing on the stage in front of your audience.

The first recommendation involved drafting in a colleague to perform your presentation for you. This provides the ideal opportunity to visualise the slides from a distance as the presentation progresses. We also suggested the use of a video camera. This achieves the important element of distance visualisation for both the presentation itself and the gestures made towards the screen and images on the slides. The review process allows critical analysis to take place in private; this is acceptable as long as you allow yourself to be critical. Self reflection is an area not to be avoided, but one that needs to be embraced when becoming a Power Presenter. Whichever method you choose it should form a basic requirement used in conjunction with the principle of rehearse, rehearse and rehearse.

Just as attention to detail and rehearsal are vital components of good presenting, so is post-presentation analysis. Knowing about the last event is one thing, but making the next one even better is a whole new ball game. In fact, you could say that the first step towards your next Power Presentation is reviewing and analysing the delivery of your last one.

Then there is the subject of live advice you can receive during your presentation. We all know that it is asking a lot to expect the presenter to be able to deliver key messages as well as to analyse the room at the same time to make sure that their presentation is as effective as possible.

Wearing a small earpiece and having a friend or colleague there to offer advice as you present can be a powerful means by which you can optimise your delivery. If you think wearing an earpiece is a step too far for the type or types of presentation you give, there is a lower tech alternative in the form of a personal assistant – someone who is there on hand to follow your presentation and to direct you as you present. They may be there just to make sure you don't 'forget you lines'. Alternatively, their role may be to provide you with live feedback as to how the presentation is going.

Yet again, the overriding point is that if there is a potential financial benefit from the presentation, consider the value of it in relation to the cost of creating and delivering absolutely the best presentation possible.

Finally, a number of presenters we've worked with confuse having a support structure with having every answer to all the questions an audience might ask them. They get all wrapped up in the matter of questions from the audience. So much so that they lose focus on the presentation itself. Our advice is that it is better to be honest with the audience and say that as a presenter you are unlikely to be able to answer every question they may have, but reassure them that you will go away and find the answers they want.

As one final thought, consider this. The world leaders of tomorrow are being forged today, they are being taught in schools, colleges and universities right now. The effectiveness of their education comes down in part to how much they learn and that means how much they remember in future. The effectiveness of the learning is in part dependent on how well the information is conveyed to them and that's about presenting. How much more important could it be?

Then there are all those business presentations. The ones where billions of pounds or dollars hang on the outcome of some presentation somewhere. Jobs depend on them, companies' very futures depend on them and again in part the very lifeblood of the economy is dependent. Once again, you see that presentations are a key attribute of modern commerce and vitally important to individuals and organisations alike.

For sure, there are many, many other types of presentation given every hour of every day. Many, many of them are of vital importance to the presenter and some are critical to the audience. Whatever the style and content, I'll wager that the value of the information is far higher than just a few minutes of bullet points on a slide.

If you have information to convey to others, then the contents of this book are aimed to help you impart it more effectively, to make it more memorable and to help you become the best communicator you can possibly be. Remember that information is the most valuable commodity a person can possess and we think being able to communicate it as a Power Presenter is just as important.

By the way, once you take on board the advice given in this book, then don't limit it to when you present. What we have covered is also at the heart of how humans communicate and so you can use the tools and techniques whenever you converse with others: With family, in a job interview, working in a store or even out on a date. The opportunities really are endless. The common denominators are people communicating with each other face-to-face and every time that occurs, aspects of the contents of this book apply. Enjoy!

About the authors

"By appreciation, we make excellence in others our own property."
Voltaire

Phillip Adcock is a leading authority on people's behaviour. With more than 30 years of human behavioural research, he has developed a unique ability to identify what it is that makes people tick, both psychologically and physiologically. He works in an advantageous position of not being constrained within any particular brain science field. Moreover, Phillip has developed his skills by combining the teachings of experts on numerous aspects of neuroscience, psychology and emotion within his professional role of helping leading brands and retailers better understand how to communicate with their customers – us.

Phillip has a passion for watching others and trying to understand why human beings do what they do. Even at school, he would observe and then analyse the interpersonal behaviour of others and himself. Phillip realised that understanding the human brain, but not being confined to any specialist viewpoint offers rewarding career opportunities.

Phillip recognised that there weren't any relevant college or university courses that would ready him for a professional life in commercial psychology or the psychology of communication. There were numerous opportunities to study a particular discipline, for example neuroscience, which was traditionally the study of the nervous system, but which has now become an interdisciplinary science involving other disciplines such as psychology, computer science, mathematics, physics, philosophy and medicine. He could have taken a more classical route and studied one of the traditional aspects of human psychology; the science and knowledge of the human brain from a point of view of relieving dysfunction and distress. Alternatively, he could have majored in business or motivational psychology; the subject of helping organisations and the individuals within them to reach their full potential by way of re-programming their brains for success.

With a real passion for understanding what makes people tick, Philip began a 30-year course of self-teaching, which has culminated in the writing of this book. In the early years Phillip worked as a retail consultant, frustrated that many shopper and staff interactions failed to meet the needs of either. Phillip identified that by understanding how the shopper wanted to be communicated to and aligning that with the approach of the store and its staff, it was possible to dramatically increase sales and market share for an ever-increasing list of the world's leading retailers and brands.

As merchandising development manager for a leading chain of stores in the UK, he again studied shoppers and their interaction and communication with staff. This entailed employing research agencies to analyse, quantify and qualify how shoppers behaved in the hundreds of stores. In addition, he was very interested in knowing more about the attitudes, needs and opinions of shoppers and how they communicated them both to staff and to professional researchers. Armed with the knowledge of how shoppers think, communicate and behave, and combining that with a unique knowledge of human emotions, he was able to develop in-store initiatives that better aligned shoppers with the ranges of products available.

In 1999, Phillip founded one of only a few specialist shopper research agencies, Shopping Behaviour Xplained Ltd (SBXL). It is now one of the leading shopping behaviour and emotions specialists, which combine a range of state-of-the-art technology and techniques with academic studies and on-going research. This approach enables SBXL to provide retailers and brands with tangible and useable data to help them optimise their communication with shoppers that will enhance sales.

Over the last 30 years, Phillip has presented to thousands and thousands of people, from CEOs of leading companies to delivering lectures at a number of universities. So he has uniquely been able to understand and develop communication from a number of different angles; from communicator to 'communicatee' (recipient).

Having spent so many years understanding how businesses and individuals communicate and like to be communicated to, combined with presenting the findings at all levels of society and commerce, it was logical for him to share his expertise with a wider audience, if for no other reason than to reduce the number of mind numbingly dull presentations that exist in the world today. So, being armed with a powerful combination of unique academic knowledge and comprehensive practical experience, Phillip Adcock has now turned his attention to the very subject of communication; specifically in relation to presentations. It is hoped that while this book provides readers with a wealth of understanding that they can incorporate into their strategic and tactical business communications, it will also provide every reader with an informative guide that will help them get more out of communicating with other human beings.

Ian Callow is an experienced director of training, which has allowed his interpersonal communication skills to develop, in conjunction with an increased understanding of a presenter's physiology. Everyday, Ian is gauging the body language of an audience to assess the level of learning that is still available.

Ian's work has allowed him to train staff within corporate companies, local authorities, Primary Health Care Trusts and universities. This has provided the opportunity to train staff of corporate clients such as HSBC, Microsoft, AstraZeneca, and Jaguar Land Rover. The diversity which this provides in relation to industry, staff and interaction means each training session needs to be adapted, similar to adapting a PowerPoint presentation as mentioned in this book. One presentation and one presentation style does not fit all. Having this variation is what Ian enjoys as an independent director of training, as it provides opportunities to study delegates and their reaction to presentations.

Ian has a thorough background in sales, marketing and training. Each of these helped to develop new skills when directing current training courses. When in account executive roles, Ian attended numerous training sessions. Although these sessions were good, Ian always left the venue wanting more information and questioning the presenters' methods. This questioning and analysing presenters and training methods has led to this book and supporting training course.

Having studied to degree level Ian moved initially into the field of marketing, where an understanding of presenting facts and figures was an integral element in presenting information to senior managers and directors. These early presentations consisted of bullet points, graphs and tables. In these early days it was an acceptable use of PowerPoint. As knowledge improved it soon became apparent that supporting notes and slides need to be treated as two entities.

Progressing into account executive roles Ian secured several monthly awards as well as a yearly award. A large proportion of this success was down to listening and reading body language from clients. This understanding and building relationships has developed the calm attitude Ian possesses whilst in the training environment. Ian encourages clients, allowing them to build confidence when presenting and developing software skills.

The account executive roles early in his career allowed Ian the opportunity to witness numerous presentations at exhibitions and conferences. The majority of these used the inevitable PowerPoint without any consideration to the delegates and their visual requirements. This analysis of people and their presentations within this environment led to frustration and the desire to make a change in attitude and skill level for the majority of presenters using PowerPoint.

Ian decided to work as an independent director of training towards the end of the 1990s when he formed ISD Training Limited. Ian has trained thousands of people from all levels of organisations from shop floor workers to board directors. The interpersonal skills required and the knowledge to adapt presentation styles for each audience has enhanced the understanding of presenting and the importance of variation. The supporting training course is an example of the variation, where clients are treated as individuals and sessions tailored to their particular development strategy. It is these skills which Ian wishes to share in writing this book and training course.

Over later years Ian has been involved in training newer technologies such as polling devices, video analysis devices and interactive whiteboard technology. Each of these will allow for greater audience participation, breaking down the presenter/trainee or presenter/delegate barrier. Ian explores these technologies within the chapters of this book and how they can improve you as a presenter.

With so much time spent in the business presentation environment Ian now feels able to convey some key messages and experiences, allowing you to release the Power Presenter within.

Thank you and enjoy your read.

Presenting excellence is a click away

By now, you are well on your way to becoming a Power Presenter, and although this book has transformed your presenting ability, we want you to go even further.

The Presenter's Handbook does not have to stop with this page. To achieve real presentation excellence why not consider a bespoke training course? These are tailored to the individual needs of you and your organisation.

Whether you want one-to-one coaching or training for entire teams or even organisations to transform their presenting ability, then we can create the ideal course.

For more information, please visit: www.presentershandbook.com or follow us on twitter @Pres_Handbook for the latest tips and advice.

PRINTED AND BOUND BY:

Copytech (UK) Limited trading as Printondemand-worldwide,
9 Culley Court, Bakewell Road, Orton Southgate. Peterborough,
PE2 6XD, United Kingdom.